Being Taoist

# Books by Eva Wong

*Cultivating Stillness*

*Cultivating the Energy of Life*

*Feng-shui*

*Harmonizing Yin and Yang*

*Holding Yin, Embracing Yang*

*Lieh-tzu*

*A Master Course in Feng-shui*

*Nourishing the Essence of Life*

*Seven Taoist Masters*

*Tales of the Dancing Dragon*

*Tales of the Taoist Immortals*

*The Tao of Health, Longevity, and Immortality*

*Taoism: An Essential Guide*

*Teachings of the Tao*

# Being Taoist

## Wisdom for Living a Balanced Life

*Edited and translated by*

## Eva Wong

Shambhala
*Boston & London*
2015

Shambhala Publications, Inc.
Horticultural Hall
300 Massachusetts Avenue
Boston, Massachusetts 02115
www.shambhala.com

9 8 7 6 5 4 3 2 1

First Edition
Printed in the United States of America

⊗ This edition is printed on acid-free paper that meets the
American National Standards Institute z39.48 Standard.
♻This book is printed on 30% postconsumer recycled paper.
For more information please visit www.shambhala.com.

Distributed in the United States by Penguin Random House LLC
and in Canada by Random House of Canada Ltd

Designed by James D. Skatges

Library of Congress Cataloging-in-Publication Data
Being Taoist: wisdom for living a balanced life / edited and translated
by Eva Wong.
pages   cm
ISBN 978-1-61180-241-2 (pbk.)
1. Spiritual life—Taoism.  I. Wong, Eva, 1951–, editor, translator.
II. Huainan zi. English. Selections.
BL1923.B36 2015
299.5'1444—dc23
2014019273

# Contents

## PART THREE

## The Taoist in Private Life
### *The Art of Concealment: Hidden Sky*

Teachings from *The Great Patriarch Laozi's Treatise on Internal Awareness*, *The Great Mysterious Grotto Precious Classic on the Subtle Method of Turning Awareness Inward*, and *The Nine Cultivations*

## PART FOUR

## The Taoist in Spirit Life
### *The Art of Being: Free and Easy Wandering*

Teachings from the *Zhuangzi*

# Introduction

## WHAT DOES IT MEAN TO BE TAOIST?

To be Taoist is to embody the wisdom of Taoism in all aspects of life: public, domestic, private, and spirit. Many Taoists participate in society as leaders, advisers, entrepreneurs, and professionals. Yet others are householders, fully engaged in family and domestic life. The stories of Taoist immortals presented in my *Tales of the Taoist Immortals* and *Tales of the Dancing Dragon* highlight the lives of Taoists in and from all walks of life. If there is one thing common among Taoists, however, it is the presence and the balance of each of these aspects of living. Not only do Taoists live these four aspects of life fully, there is also an outlook and an art to moving through each of them.

Central to the public life of the Taoist is the art of leadership. Leadership is not about controlling and forcing things to go our way or dragging everybody else behind us. Rather, it is inspiring and leading by example. The outlook that forms the foundation of the art of leadership is known as the *view of vastness.*

Central to the domestic life of the Taoist is the art of healthy living. Healthy living means appreciating the life force of the body and nourishing it with a healthy diet and healthy active lifestyle. It also means not wasting life energy by indulging in extravagances and overworking

1

body and mind. The outlook that forms the foundation of the art of healthy living is called *embracing simplicity.*

Central to the private life of the Taoist is the art of concealment. In Taoism, to conceal does not mean to be aloof and disengaged. Rather, it means not to dazzle or make ourselves the focus of attention. Our modern culture encourages us to brag about our achievements and show off our wealth. Contrary to displaying their talents and abilities, Taoists cloak their knowledge, and even their wisdom, using them only at the appropriate place and time. The outlook that forms the foundation of the art of concealment is called *hidden sky,* which means concealing the skylike vastness of our wisdom rather than basking in its glory.

Central to the spirit life of the Taoist is the art of being. The art of being touches every aspect of our lived experience. The outlook that forms the foundation of the art of being is *free and easy wandering,* a phrase from the Taoist classic *Zhuangzi* that refers to the playful journey of a completely liberated consciousness through the limitless expanse of the Tao.

The aim of this book is not only to show that to be Taoist is to live fully in the public, domestic, private, and spirit sectors of life, but also to challenge us to stop, reflect, and ask ourselves: Do we balance the public, domestic, private, and spirit aspects of our lives? Do we emphasize some at the expense of the others? Do we ever think about unifying worldly and spiritual wisdom in our lives? If you haven't considered these questions before, I hope that you will as you read this book.

## GIVING VOICE TO A TEXT

Taoist texts are meant to be practical. The goal of any Taoist text is to help people to be better individuals and to make the world a more harmonious and peaceful place. After all, the Taoist classic that started the spiritual tradition of Taoism is titled the *Tao Te Ching (Daodejing). Tao* means the "natural way," and *te* means "virtue." Together, they indicate that the path of Taoism is about following what is natural and embodying what is virtuous.

The teachings of Taoism are meant to be accessible and relevant. However, although wisdom is timeless, the language in which teachings are presented is tied to historical and social contexts. What was common knowledge in one historical period could become obtuse in another. Moreover, when we take the wisdom of one culture and translate it into another, nuances in language and subtle cultural references can become mind-boggling. To make the Taoist teachings accessible to the non-Chinese reader, I have taken the approach of "giving voice to a text"—a phrase I first used in my translation of the work *Lieh-tzu.*

In giving voice to a text, the goal is not to translate verbatim but to take excerpts that contain the essence of the teachings and make them relevant and easy to understand. References to obscure incidents in Chinese history and difficult-to-pronounce Chinese names are therefore kept to a minimum here, and linguistic subtleties particular to literary styles of certain historical periods are rendered into modern language.

Every text has a voice, especially the sacred texts of wisdom traditions. The voice of the text carries the intention of the author and gives life to the text, allowing us, as readers, to enter an intimate and meaningful relationship with the author and the work. To enter a relationship with a text, we must first understand that the teachings are carried not only in the semantics of a text but also in the voice that communicates them. Second, we need to become listeners, not analysts and critics. Third, we need to suspend our personal beliefs and opinions as we relate to the text.

*[margin notes: many levels · listen · NON Judge — Mental]*

Fourth, in listening to the voice of a text, we need to regard the text as another being. This means that the text is not an object to be read by us, the subject. Rather, we are listening to another subject: a friend, teacher, adviser, or mentor. In this way, we can begin to develop a respect for the text and eventually learn from it. The approach of "listening" to a text is called *hermeneutics*, a technique pioneered by the German philosopher Martin Heidegger and developed further by more recent European philosophers such as Paul Ricoeur and Hans-Georg Gadamer. Further discussion of the hermeneutics of listening can be found in the introduction to my translation of *Lieh-tzu.*

*[margin notes: listen to this teacher]*

In this book, each of the four aspects of being Taoist is communicated through a different voice.

The essence of public life lies in the art of leadership. Who can teach us leadership and its place in public life? Who can show us the view of vastness that is the mark of a true leader? It is the voice of the sages.

*[margin notes: leadership sages]*

What kind of voice is this? It is a formal voice that is soft and patient, teaching us the nature of the Tao—the nature of reality, cosmology, and virtue. When we listen to this voice, it is as if we are sitting with fellow students in a large hall or courtyard, listening to a group of sages giving discourses on these teachings.

The essence of domestic life lies in the art of healthy living. Who can advise us on how to live a healthy lifestyle? Who can show us the principle of embracing simplicity? It is the voice of a mentor. What kind of voice is this? It is the intimate and caring voice of a friend and adviser. The guidance from our mentor comes from wisdom that is developed through a lifetime of experience; it is not something gleaned from books. When we listen to this voice, it is as if we are sitting on our back porch or in our kitchen with someone we trust.

The essence of private life lies in the art of concealment and its shadow, revelation. Who can teach us how to appreciate and fully live an inner life of meditation and contemplative stillness? Who can show us how to direct our awareness toward the vast hidden sky that is our own consciousness? It is the voice of a spiritual teacher. What kind of voice is this? It is the firm yet compassionate voice that communicates clear instructions on how to experience our limitless consciousness. When we listen to this voice, it is as if we are sitting on a meditation cushion in a peaceful, quiet, and spacious room listening to the words of a respected teacher.

The essence of spirit life lies in the art of being. Who can show us how to have a spirit life that is alive, playful, and unencumbered? Who can guide us to experience total freedom and wander free and easy through diverse realities? It is the voice of the immortal, a realized being. What kind of voice is this? It is an ephemeral voice, an elusive voice, a voice that delights in one instance and shocks in the next, a voice that can break us out of our self-imposed limitations and help us enter realms that we have never experienced. When we listen to this voice, it is as if we are in the presence of realized beings. Expounding the teachings in unconventional ways through stories, musings, conversations, and discourse, the voice of the immortal leads us away from linear thought and habitual feelings. Free from conventionality, the teachings plunge us, the listeners, into a state in which the duality of the teacher and the taught is dissolved.

## THE ART OF LEADERSHIP THROUGH
## THE VOICE OF THE SAGE

To carry the voice of the sage, I have chosen excerpts from the *Huainanzi*, a text compiled by a prince of the early part of the Han Dynasty (206 B.C.E.–220 C.E.). The prince ruled the fiefdom of Huainan and became known as Huainanzi, the sage of Huainan. Huainanzi was a patron of Taoist practitioners: scholars, alchemists, diviners, herbalists, and magicians. Often he would invite Taoists to give talks on topics such as the nature of the Tao, the nature of reality, and the importance of virtue in leadership and everyday life. The book *Huainanzi* is a compilation of these teachings.

Because the prince ruled a small kingdom and was a member of the Han royal family, the main focus of the collected teachings was on how to lead and govern in an enlightened way. Huainanzi himself was a public figure, accustomed to administering a state, enforcing laws, maintaining public safety, and taking care of the citizens. For these reasons, the book *Huainanzi* is the most suitable text for expounding the art of leadership in the public life of a Taoist.

The key to leadership is the view of vastness. For the prince of Huainan, a leader must embrace an outlook that is vast and limitless. Small view and pettiness have no place in the mind of a leader. The enlightened leader is one who allows things to run their natural course instead of imposing his or her will on them. Just as the Tao benefits and accommodates all, the leader thinks and acts for the good of all. Knowing that ambition creates disharmony, the leader does not push him- or herself and others beyond the limits of physical strength and mental ability.

To maintain a view of vastness, a leader needs to understand the nature of reality and the interdependency of all things. In the natural order, yin and yang are balanced. The leader observes the natural world, understands its transient nature, intuits that which is constant, and acts in harmony with all of it. Policies are made with a sensitivity to changes in the seasons, the cycles of waxing and waning of the five elements (metal, wood, water, fire, and earth), and the rise and fall of yin and yang.

The thoughts and actions of an enlightened leader are founded on virtue. If a leader embraces virtue, there will be no need for harsh laws, cold justice, debates on ethics, and rule by consensus. Instead of benefiting small but powerful interests, policies would be made to benefit all. In the words of *Huainanzi*, in countries that are led by enlightened leaders, "warhorses will be retired to roam the pastures, and soldiers can return home to farm and make furniture." In our day and age, this is equivalent to saying that lobbyists will disappear and there won't be a need for standing armies or even peacekeeping forces.

For the prince of Huainan, the essence of leadership lies in embracing virtue and being connected to the Tao. A leader acts by not forcing, leads by not bragging, and commands respect by not threatening. Finally, the highest act of a leader is to leave with no trace when his or her work is done.

## THE ART OF HEALTHY LIVING THROUGH THE VOICE OF THE MENTOR

To carry the voice of the mentor, I have chosen excerpts from three texts: *Principles of Nourishing Life and Cultivating Longevity* (*Yansheng Yanming Lu*), written in the fifth century by Tao Hongjing; *Peng Zu's Method of Prolonging Life* (*Peng Zu's Shesheng Yanxing Lun*), collected and edited by Tao Hongjing; and *Embracing Simplicity* (*Baopuzi*), written by Ge Hong, a fourth-century alchemist.

Tao Hongjing and Ge Hong were householders. Both had families, and both lived an active domestic life while practicing the arts of health and longevity. Ge Hong was an alchemist and herbalist, known for his research into the use of herbs and minerals to improve health and prolong life. Tao Hongjing was a personal friend and adviser to an emperor as well as one of the foremost exponents of the Shangqing (High Clarity) lineage of Taoism. Shangqing Taoists believed that one should care for the body in the same way an enlightened ruler cares for his or her subjects. Therefore, they advocate eating healthy foods, having a healthy sexual life, and living simply. For them, embracing simplicity was the ultimate way to conserve life energy and live a healthy and long life. For this reason, the writings of Tao Hongjing and Ge Hong are ideal for expounding the art of healthy living in the domestic life of the Taoist.

The key to healthy living is embracing simplicit[...] householder understands and appreciates the energy o[...] fore lives in moderation and contentment in order [...] nourish qi, or life energy. If we are not extravagant an[...] have fewer desires. With fewer desires, we will become [...] gain and loss. Being less anxious over gain and loss, we will be less likely to push ourselves to get more and have more. By integrating a healthy *life energy* diet, healthy sexual habits, and contentment into our domestic life, we will be able to preserve and cultivate our qi more effectively. Balancing action with nonaction, movement with stillness, we will be less likely to abuse body and mind. Having a peaceful disposition and being kind and helpful, we will not develop negative attitudes that will drain life energy.

Healthy living is simple and straightforward. If we eat nutritious foods in moderation, and have a balanced diet of proteins, grains, and fruits, we will be physically strong and mentally clear. Don't be stuck in one form of diet throughout your life. Be open to changes in diet through the seasons. Moods, aging, and level of physical health and mental clarity can also affect how and what we eat. Doing physical exercise such as qigong and gentle forms of martial arts can relax body and mind and improve the circulation of energy in the body. Most important, listen to the body like an enlightened ruler attending to the welfare of the people.

In Taoism, sexual arousal and activity are considered part and parcel of being human. The Tao is made of one yin and one yang, and it is said that all things are created from the copulation of yin and yang. Plants and animals procreate naturally, so why not humans? It is only when sexual desire becomes possessive and aggressive that procreative energy drains faster than it can be cultivated. A healthy sexual lifestyle is one in which natural sexual urges are satisfied, energy is neither hoarded nor wasted, and we know how to replenish sexual energy after expending it.

Finally, to embrace simplicity is to delight in household activities such as cooking, eating a good meal, caring for loved ones, enjoying the sexual company of a partner, nourishing the body by doing gentle exercise, and freeing the mind from anxiety and negativity by knowing contentment.

## THE ART OF CONCEALMENT THROUGH
## THE VOICE OF THE SPIRITUAL TEACHER

To carry the voice of the spiritual teacher, I have chosen three texts: *The Great Patriarch Laozi's Treatise on Internal Awareness* (*Taishang Laojun Neiguanjing*), written in the fifth century; *The Great Mysterious Grotto Precious Classic on the Subtle Method of Turning Awareness Inward* (*Taishang Dongxuan Lingbao Guanmiao Jing*), written in the ninth century; and *The Nine Cultivations* (*Jiu Shao*), written sometime between the eighth and tenth centuries. The authors are unknown, but the last two texts show the influence of the teachings of Shangqing Taoist Sima Zhengzhen (646–735) on meditation.

The texts describe three steps of Taoist meditation as originally taught in the Shangqing lineage, but this form of meditation has long been adopted by other major Taoist lineages such as the Quanzhen (Complete Reality) lineage and the Xiantianwujimen (Primordial Limitless Gate) lineage. The private life of the Taoist is inner life, and inner life is illuminated by meditation, which in the Shangqing tradition means turning our awareness inward. When we are too occupied with the world outside, our private or inner life suffers, because we have no time to tune our awareness into our own consciousness and discover its richness.

The Shangqing method of meditation is called *neiguan*. *Nei* means "inner," and *guan* means "view." *Neiguan* meditation is about turning our awareness inward to experience our consciousness. The word *guan* has often been mistranslated as "gazing" or "observing." Although this fits the mundane usage of the word, in the Shangqing instructions, *guan* is about having a view, an orientation. Therefore, meditation is about becoming aware of consciousness, not watching or gazing at it. When we tune our awareness to our thoughts and experience them directly, we are totally involved. When we are merged with thought and nonthought, the duality of subject and object disappears.

In contrast, if we observe or look at our thoughts, we become bystanders. Worse, we often end up being critics and analysts, and the duality of watcher (subject) and thought (object) is never dissolved. If we understand that we are not watchers, and that fundamentally there is no watcher and watched, we will be able to relax and flow with the activity and nonactivity of consciousness.

In Taoist meditation, the first step is to turn our awareness inward toward the life of consciousness. Most people are so occupied by the external world that they don't realize that there is a very rich world within themselves. In this stage, we relax, let go, and learn to appreciate that we have an internal universe. Within this internal universe is our consciousness, our life force, and a body that is like a nation—with provinces (head, neck, abdomen, arms, legs, and so on), fertile fields that cultivate and store life energy (the internal organs), and an infrastructure that carries nutrients to nourish every part of the body (the arteries, veins, lymphatic system, and so on).

After we have learned to tune our awareness to the internal world, we are ready for the second step, to heighten that awareness. Heightening awareness means that our awareness becomes more sophisticated and more discerning. Rather than just noticing that we have qi (or energy) and thoughts, we begin to experience subtle nuances of periods of thought and nonthought, to feel how qi moves through our bodies, and to identify which areas are blocked and which are healthy.

Finally, after developing a heightened awareness of our inner world, we are ready for the third step, to turn the awareness outward to the external world. The insight that we have experienced in meditation is brought into everyday life to benefit the world and the people around us.

The essence of these three steps, or stages, of meditation is embodied in the meaning of *hidden sky*. Indeed, Hidden Sky (Tianyin) is the Taoist name of Sima Zhengzhen, who was responsible for developing this form of meditation. To be hidden means to be concealed, and concealment is defined by its complement, revelation. Thus, the key to concealment is knowing when to hide by turning inward and when to reveal by turning outward. Consciousness is likened to the vastness of the sky. This sky is vast, but it is also hidden, and its mystery and power can be discovered and experienced only by turning our awareness toward it.

## THE ART OF BEING THROUGH
## THE VOICE OF THE IMMORTAL

To carry the voice of the immortal, I have chosen excerpts from the *Zhuangzi*. The book *Zhuangzi* is divided into three sections: the inner, the outer, and the miscellaneous chapters. The inner chapters were written in the third century B.C.E. by Zhuangzi himself. The outer and miscellaneous chapters were written by various Taoists inspired by Zhuangzi between the second century B.C.E. and the fourth century C.E.

I have translated excerpts from all the chapters of the *Zhuangzi*. Despite diverse authorship, they have common themes: freeing ourselves from boundaries created by petty thoughts and actions, exploring the wealth of consciousness by wandering its vastness, never being separated from virtue, and following the natural way.

The contents of the *Zhuangzi* are often disjointed, with little continuity even within each chapter. In giving voice to the *Zhuangzi* as the immortal, I have decided not only to translate but also to edit the chapters, presenting the material in a more coherent way while preserving the spirit of the teachings.

The teachings of the *Zhuangzi* are the most quintessential of Taoism. They show us the spirit life of the Taoist, one who floats with the times; transcends the limitations of even space; and merges with the sky, the earth, and humanity. Spirit is limitless. Without a spirit life, we are forever bound by limits. Even if we live healthily, practice the arts of longevity, and rest in the emptiness and stillness of meditation, we are still living in a world of forms and limits. The *Zhuangzi* is about experiencing and living in the formless and the limitless. Until we have embraced this last aspect of being Taoist, we are not really being Taoist.

## THE ART OF BEING TAOIST

The art of being Taoist is about balancing, integrating, and unifying worldly and spiritual wisdom. Public, domestic, private, and spirit lives support and enrich one another. Not embracing all of them means robbing ourselves of much of the richness that life can offer.

A leader should have not only a public life but also fully developed domestic, private, and spirit lives. The domestic life teaches the leader to be caring and intimate. Without domesticity, leadership can become cold and impersonal. Moreover, we need to be able to care for our health before we can care for family, friends, and community. The private life gives the leader a heightened awareness of both the internal and external world, so that critical decisions can be made with clarity. The spirit life teaches the leader what it means to be a leader: to hold a vast view, be free of conceptual bonds, move with the times, think and act in virtue, and leave without a trace when the work is done.

A householder should have not only a domestic life but also fully developed public, private, and spirit lives. The public life teaches the householder the importance of caring for others in addition to providing for the immediate family. Without public responsibility, domestic life can become stifled and self-centered. Focusing solely on personal and family matters can blind us to the needs of society and the world. The private life teaches the householder to cultivate health, longevity, and mental clarity, so that livelihood and domestic concerns do not drain life energy. The spirit life teaches the householder what it means to live in a household: to care but not possess, to hold the bigger view and not be bogged down by small concerns, and to think and act from virtue instead of personal wants.

A practitioner of meditation should have not only a private life but also fully developed public, domestic, and spirit lives. The public life helps the practitioner not to be obsessed with his or her own enlightenment and thus forget that the goal of spiritual practice is to lead others toward enlightenment. The domestic life reminds the spiritual practitioner that household activities cultivate spirituality. Domestic tasks such as cooking, washing dishes, cleaning, and making home repairs bring spiritual practice into everyday activity. Domestic life grounds spiritual practice in the ordinary, reminding us that enlightenment is an ordinary experience attainable by all. The spirit life brings luminosity and radiance into spiritual practice. Spirit life takes techniques from the relative world (such as meditation and *qigong*) and connects them to the ultimate reality. It is through spirit life that the practitioner merges with the vast and primordial oneness of the Tao.

An immortal should have not only a spirit life but also fully developed public, domestic, and private lives. Many immortals live in the earthly realm, mingling with mortals. Zhang Boduan (987–1082), the founder of the southern Quanzhen (Complete Reality) lineage of Taoism, said, "Lesser immortals conceal themselves in the mountains and forests; greater immortals conceal themselves in small towns; the greatest immortals conceal themselves in large cities." What he meant was that the more realized the individual, the less a retreatlike environment will be needed to support his or her practice. The public life provides a vehicle for an immortal to use his or her virtue to help the world. When immortals live a public life, they are leaders or advisers to leaders. The domestic life provides a vehicle for an immortal to practice humility by doing household chores like any ordinary person. It was said that the immortal Liezi (fourth century B.C.E.) cleaned his home, cooked for his wife, and fed the pigs. The private life provides a vehicle for the immortal to continue to cultivate and nourish the energy of life.

In the Taoist tradition, to integrate the public, domestic, private, and spirit lives is to live life to its fullest. Since all things emanate from the Tao, we are all connected. The thoughts and actions of one person, the movement of one pebble on the earth, or a single leaf falling from one tree can send ripples around the world, affecting everything far and near, present and future. The art of living is about understanding and living this interdependency so that we can help others to connect to the natural and virtuous ways of the Tao.

To be Taoist is to embody the principles of yin and yang and simultaneously live a worldly and spiritual life. In public life and domestic life, we embody the principle of yang, weaving worldly wisdom into our lives. In private life and spirit life, we embody the principle of yin, weaving spiritual wisdom into our lives. When these four sectors of life are fully integrated, we are the living embodiment of the consummate balance of yin and yang.

To be Taoist is to become the very essence of the five elements: fire, wood, earth, water, and metal. In public life we are virtuous leaders. Holding a vision with wisdom and maturity, we inspire others and lead with enthusiasm and humility. We become the element fire that surges upward, always reaching for the vastness that is the sky. In domestic life, we are healthy householders. Caring and contented, we celebrate our health and well-being and enjoy family, friends, and life at home. We become the element wood that grows deep into the ground, always drawing on the homely wisdom that is practical and down-to-earth. In private life we enjoy the richness of our vast consciousness. Embracing stillness, emptiness, clarity, and ordinariness, we welcome alike action and nonaction, movement and rest, chaos and order. We become the element earth, at times dull and inert, and at times colorful and unpredictable. In spirit life we are never separated from the mysterious sacredness of the world around us. Our limitless spirit holds all diversities, resolves all conflicts, and accommodates everything. Participating fully in the dance of consciousness and experiencing its beauty, mystery, and vastness, we are committed in everything we do, knowing that beyond the limits of understanding there is depth and power. We become the element water, always following a natural course, changing with the world and yet changing the world.

When these four sectors of life are balanced and integrated, we become the element metal. Like a sword tempered by fire and water, we are strong and flexible. Like precious minerals, we are continuously nourished and transformed by the womb of the earth. Like a chisel in harmony with a block of wood, we carve and create all that is beautiful, mysterious, and sacred.

## PART ONE

# The Taoist in Public Life

*The Art of Leadership: The View of Vastness*

Teachings from the *Huainanzi*

# 1

# The Natural Way

## THE TAO

The Tao envelops the sky, covers the earth, and extends beyond the four directions. Its height cannot be measured, and its depth cannot be fathomed. It embraces the universe and gives birth to all things. Like water gushing from a spring, it flows everywhere and penetrates everything. Rising and falling, swirling and churning, it separates yin from yang, earth from sky, and muddy from clear. Stand it up, and it can hold the sky and support the earth; lay it down, and it can circle the oceans. Time does not affect it. Use does not exhaust it. Expand it, and it will fill the vastness of space; shrink it, and you can hold it in your hand. Depending on the circumstances, it can be small or large, dim or bright, weak or strong, soft or hard, and crooked or straight.

The Tao embraces the sky and the earth. It harmonizes yin and yang and maintains the balance in nature. Time and space exist because of it. The sun, the moon, and the stars shine because of it. In it, softness realizes its fullest potential and subtleties achieve their greatest limits. Because of it, the mountains are high, the seas are deep, animals run, and birds fly. The Tao has no form or shape, but its power is endless. All things are created from it, but in creating and nourishing the myriad things, its energy is not exhausted.

The Tao is simple yet profound. Rising, it does not gain height; falling, it does not flatten out. Multiply it, and it does not increase; subtract from it, and it does not decrease; divide it, and it does not diminish. Strike it, and it is not injured; excavate it, and it does not deepen; fill it, and it is not raised.

The Tao is elusive and intangible. Look for it, and it cannot be found; listen to it, and it cannot be heard. It is as ungraspable as space and as deep as a cavern, but it resonates to every change in the universe. It stretches out when it needs to expand; it contracts when it needs to be small. Rising with yang and sinking with yin, it can be high or low, long or short, round or square, curved or straight. Because it has no definite shape and form, it can adjust to every possible situation and blend with every conceivable condition in the universe.

The Tao gives birth to all things but is not consumed by them. It is responsible for their growth but does not direct their destiny. Mammals, reptiles, amphibians, fish, birds, and insects live because of the natural way of the Tao, but they do not feel indebted to it. They die because of the natural way of the Tao, but they do not blame or resent it. Animals appear to have a better understanding of the Tao than we humans do, because we praise the Tao when we succeed and curse it when we fail.

Water lilies are rooted in water, and trees are rooted in the earth. Birds fly in the sky, mammals run on the earth, fish swim in the waters, and tigers and leopards prowl in the mountains. This is the natural way of things. Rub two pieces of wood against each other, and you will have fire. Heat metal with fire, and the metal will lose its shape. Round objects spin on the surface of water, and hollow objects float. Such are the laws of nature.

When the spring wind blows, soft rains fall to nourish the earth. In the season of growth, birds lay eggs and mammals give birth. Leaves sprout and flowers bloom. No one has to tell the trees to grow and the animals to procreate, because this is the natural way of things. When the autumn wind blows, frost covers the ground. In the season of waning, leaves wither and fall. Mammals and birds feed constantly, building the energy that will help them survive the winter. Insects and reptiles hide beneath the earth. Trees shed their leaves and send their energy into the roots. Fish swim to the bottom of lakes. Life seems to disappear from nature, but no one is responsible for the disappearance.

Birds build nests, sea creatures hide in underwater caves, mammals rest on beds of grass, and humans build houses. On land we travel on wheels; at sea we use a boat. Tribes in the north trap animals for fur; people in the south grow cotton. Each group adapts to its environment and develops the skills necessary for its survival. This is the natural way of things.

Many people plant trees without knowing the principles of yin and yang. They do not know that trees native to the south will wither if they are planted in the north. Not understanding the nature of plants, they are surprised when the trees die. Similarly, people who try to raise wild animals in captivity do not know that wild animals do not reproduce when they are removed from their natural habitats. Not understanding the nature of animals, they are surprised when the animals do not mate.

It is natural for oxen to have horns and for horses to have manes, but it is unnatural for them to wear halters and bridles. To force animals to wear these contraptions is an example of human effort disrupting the natural way. When something is forced to live against the natural way, it will not survive. It is for this reason that we should not impose our values and beliefs on peoples of other cultures.

Of all the things in the world, nothing is softer than water. Water is accommodating and yielding, but its depth cannot be plumbed and its boundaries cannot be measured. Rising to the sky, it becomes rain and mist. Falling to earth, it becomes springs and underground lakes. Life cannot exist without water, and crops cannot be cultivated without it. Water benefits all and has no favorites. It nourishes the smallest insect and the largest mammal and does not expect gratitude. It enriches the world and does not begrudge those who use it.

Water is soft yet strong. Strike it, and it cannot be injured. Pierce it, and it cannot be punctured. Grasp it, and it cannot be held. Its strength can wear down stone and metal. Its sustenance can nourish the whole world. It can float in the sky as clouds, squeeze through narrow valleys as streams, and spread across wide-open plains as lakes. It takes from the earth and gives back to the earth. Unbiased and nonjudgmental, it does not have notions of first and last and does not distinguish between us and them. Everything is equal in its eyes. Separating and merging, it blends with its surroundings and is at one with the sky and the earth. Not conforming to the left or the right, it can be straight or meandering. Not restrained by space and time, it can be present at the beginning and the end of all things.

The Tao is like water because it is soft and smooth. Its softness and weakness can overcome the hard and the strong. We do not know where water comes from and where it may go. We only know that even though it does not act, it benefits the whole world.

The Tao cannot be confined in shape and form because the formless is the creator of all things. If we are alienated from the Source, we will lose our connection to the Tao. Stillness is a manifestation of virtue, and softness is the foundation of the Tao. If we respect and seek it with diligence, we can return to the void and the source of creation. The void is the One that is united with all things. It stands alone, yet its greatness extends everywhere. Above, it reaches beyond the center and the eight directions. Below, it penetrates the eight levels of the earth. It is not concerned with petty details but is aware of the totality of all things. It embraces the sky and the earth and is the gateway to all principles. Its virtue is pure. It nourishes everything and cannot be exhausted.

Look for it, and it cannot be seen. Listen for it, and it cannot be heard. Try to touch it, and it cannot be felt. Although it is formless, all things exist because of it. Although it has no flavor, the five flavors are developed from it. Although it has no color, the five colors originate from it. Therefore, it is said that all things emerge from nothingness and that substance originates from the insubstantial. Although the myriad things differ in shape and form, they all come from the same origin. There are five notes in the (pentatonic) musical scale, yet no two pieces of music are identical. There are five basic flavors, yet all foods taste different. There are five basic colors, but their combinations generate a large variety of hues. Whether it is sound, flavor, or color, once the Origin is known, the rest can be created.

The Tao is at the center of all creation. It reaches the four directions and connects the sky and the earth. The purity of the Tao is like a piece of uncarved jade. When it first emerges, it appears muddy. Then with time it becomes clear and fills the empty spaces. When still, it is as still as the waters of a deep lake. When it moves, it is as elusive as the floating clouds. It is there and yet not there. It exists and yet does not exist. The Tao is where all things gather. All events emanate from it. The Tao moves in an unpredictable manner and changes in a mysterious way. It leaves no tracks and casts no shadows. It starts off behind but arrives first.

## ENLIGHTENED LEADERSHIP

Sagely rulers govern without government and lead without being leaders.

The ancient sages Fu Xi and Shen Nong understood the Tao. They ruled with benevolence and brought peace and harmony to the people. During their time (in the third millennium B.C.E.), there were no bad omens and disasters. The earth was stable, the stars moved in an orderly manner, and the seasons were timely. These sagely rulers were at one with everything. They flowed with the natural way and appeared and disappeared with the beginning and the end of things. Like clouds that move with the wind, rain, and thunder, they were never at odds with the natural way. Like spirits from other realms, they came like a dragon descending and went like a phoenix rising.

Fu Xi and Shen Nong nourished the energy of life. Their bones were strong, their meridians were open, and energy moved through their bodies like a wheel that is always turning. They did not abandon their original nature even though they were cultured. They embraced simplicity and did not indulge in luxury. They understood the meaning of hidden virtue and did not display their accomplishments in order to seek recognition. They came without fanfare, taught without claiming credit, and departed without a trace.

The virtue of Fu Xi and Shen Nong supported the sky, enriched the earth, and harmonized yin and yang. It regulated the seasons and allowed spring, summer, autumn, and winter to follow a timely course. It maintained the balance of the five elements and allowed metal, wood, water, fire, and earth to interact harmoniously. It nourished life, watered the plants, and moistened metal and stone. It made animals strong and swift, their fur soft and shiny, and their plumage thick and bright. During the sages' tenure of leadership, there were no miscarriages, stillborns, or birth defects. There were no orphans and widows, no wars and disasters. So great was the virtue of Fu Xi and Shen Nong that they not only brought peace and harmony to humanity but also maintained the balance of nature.

The sagely leaders who embraced the Tao had a particular way of governing their country. They covered their ears and did not listen to gossip; they covered their eyes and were not confused by illusions. They took away the glamour and splendor, followed the principles of the Tao, refrained from scheming, and lived in harmony with the citizens. They kept a simple agenda and aimed for the small; they minimized desire and were not burdened by attachments.

Peng Yi was a spirit who knew the workings of yin and yang. An accomplished chariot driver, he steered his vehicle in a unique way. His chariot was thunder, and his horses were the clouds and the rainbows. He rode on the mist and flew to the outermost reaches of the sky. As he traveled farther and farther into other realms, his driving skill improved, until he could journey to the limits of the eight directions. Peng Yi was one with the forces of nature. He could walk on the snow and leave no footprints. Even the sun could cast no shadow on him. Moving like a spiral on a ram's horn, he rose with the wind and floated over the grasslands, lakes, and mountains. When he descended to the ground, the earth embraced him, and when he ascended to the sky, the stars received him.

Many tried to compete with Peng Yi. Although they had light carriages and fast horses, they could not catch up with him. For Peng Yi had embraced the Tao and was at one with everything. The sky was his canopy, the earth was his chariot, and the seasons were his horses. He rode on the vapor of the clouds, flew through the skies, and became one with the Source. Traveling leisurely at his own speed, he ran with the sun, the moon, and the stars. The rain spirit swept his path and the wind spirit cleared his trails. His whip was lightning and his wheels were thunder. Above, he wandered in the emptiness and stillness of the great expanse. Below, he penetrated the great gate of the formless and rootless. His thoughts were clear, his senses keen, and nothing escaped his scrutiny. He embraced the Tao, preserved his life force, and cultivated his spirit.

Although he ventured far beyond the four directions, he always returned to the Origin. Because the sky was his shelter, he was not constricted. Because the earth was his carriage, he was not encumbered. Because the seasons were his horses, he traveled with the cycles of time. Because yin and yang were his guides, he could traverse the sky and earth with ease. And because he was at one with the source of all things, Peng Yi could fly with the stars and travel to the ends of the universe and not be tired. He did not need to strain his limbs or bend his thoughts to penetrate the mysteries of the sky or reach the boundaries of the earth. Because he understood the workings of the Tao, he could wander in the expanse of the limitless and see into the sacredness of all things.

The ground underneath our feet is strong and firm because it is content to be at the bottom of things. Water can run fast because it is content to flow down and has no desire to climb up. It is said that in ancient times, when King Shun farmed in a certain region, one year later the farmers there chose the poor plots and left the rich ones for others. When he fished in a certain river, one year later all the fishermen chose unfavorable fishing sites and left the favorable ones to others. When Shun lived among the people, he did not need to make speeches to win their support. This was because his actions spoke for themselves. When Shun ruled his kingdom, vassals sent him tribute, unruly clans became respectable, and the citizens were honest and content. He never issued orders, yet his subjects were upright and virtuous. He never passed strict laws, yet there was order and harmony.

The key to good government lies in the quality of leadership. If the leader is not virtuous, the rest of the government will simply be an unwieldy bureaucracy. If things are allowed to follow the natural way, we will not need to create organizations to run them. The sagely rulers realized that good government means being connected to the root of all things. Acting in accordance with the natural way, they did not need to create an image of themselves in front of the people. Because they refrained from scheming, they were able to preserve their spirits. Because they abstained from thoughts and actions that injure the body, they were able to live long and healthy lives. Because they cultivated stillness and followed the way of nonaction, they were able to rule without the complexity of bureaucracy. Because they followed the natural way, they could govern by not governing and act by not acting.

## KNOWING YOUR LIMITS

Know your limits, embrace softness, and abandon force. Some people fail to catch fish even though they are skilled at fishing. Others only have to drop a net into the water and fish will swim toward it. Some people fail to bring home prey even though they are skilled hunters. Others only have to put a cage on the ground and animals will be lured into it. Novices succeed when the experts fail because experts often rely on technical know-how and abandon intuition. In contrast, novices are more likely to be in tune with the workings of the Tao because they are not blinded by the tricks of the trade. As a result, they succeed where the experts fail.

The natural way is simple and clear. Human effort, however, is forced and unnecessarily complex. Human effort relies on tricks and know-how. It bows to social convention and is mixed up in the mud and dust of the world. People who live according to natural ways are at one with the vastness of the Tao, whereas those who live according to petty and fixed ways are forever imprisoned by rules.

A sharp eye can see grains of sand embedded in a rock but cannot detect fish in deep waters. A keen ear can discriminate the difference in timbre between two flutes but cannot hear the sound of thunder a hundred miles away. A talented carpenter working alone can build a cabin but not a warehouse. This is because skill, ability, and talent have limits. The ways of the Tao, however, are limitless. If we follow its principles, then even a monumental task like bringing peace and harmony to the world will not be difficult. The great King Yu of the Xia Dynasty (2070–1600 B.C.E.) could turn back the flood waters because he understood the nature of water. Shen Nong knew how to use herbs as medicine because he understood the nature of plants. The sages were able to accomplish things that were deemed impossible not because they possessed technical expertise but because they understood the Tao and the natural way.

There was once a ruler who built a thirty-foot wall around his capital. As soon as the wall was completed, the nobles rebelled and the neighboring kingdoms invaded. Seeing what was happening, his son dismantled the wall, burned the weapons, disbanded the troops, and shared his wealth with the citizens. Immediately the invasions stopped, the nobles pledged loyalty, and diplomats from the neighboring kingdoms arrived with gifts and tribute.

If you use force against others, you cannot expect them to respect you. Designing heavy armor encourages the forging of sharp swords, and building city walls will only result in the construction of siege machines. If you try to flush out muddy water with clear water, you will only churn up more dirt. If a whip is used to tame a horse and a stick is used to train a dog, even the greatest animal handlers will fail. However, if there is no cruelty or domination in your heart, even a hungry tiger will follow you home obediently.

It is difficult to explain the vastness of the ocean to a fish living in a puddle, and it is impossible to describe frost and snow to summer insects. Similarly, it is hard to discuss the Tao with people who are imprisoned in their narrow minds.

Skilled swimmers often drown, and skilled riders often fall. This is because people with skill are more likely to push their limits and risk themselves. In contrast, people without skill usually know their limits and do not expose themselves to danger. The more you want to achieve, the more you will be willing to take risks. If you are content, you will not feel the need to push yourself. As a result, you will have more time to enjoy what you already have.

Once a man named Kong thought that his strength could win a kingdom. He butted his head against a mountain and tried to push it out of his way. But before he could complete his task, he slipped and fell into the sea and drowned. His clan was defeated, and none of his descendants survived. Therefore, success and failure depend not on effort and scheming but on knowing one's limits and abilities.

Those who embrace the Tao are soft and strong. They hide their courage and do not impose their will on others. They appear powerless and inactive but are fast and efficient when they are required to act. They hold onto stillness, maintain a low profile, and do not appear unique and outstanding. Therefore, they are able to blend with the times, hold on to their own principles, and live for a long time.

Transform softness into hardness. Transform weakness into strength. Keep it changing all the time. In this way, you will understand the unity of things and be able to overcome the many with the few. Be decisive when you act. Counter adversity with calmness. If you want to be hard, you must learn to be soft. If you want to be strong, you must know what it means to be weak. Cultivate softness, and it will become hard. Cultivate weakness, and it will become strong. You can predict people's fortunes by looking at how much they can yield. The strong may be able to overcome the weak but will lose their advantage if they encounter others who are stronger. If you hide your strength, you will always be at an advantage because your opponent cannot estimate how strong you are.

The sage holds on to the stillness of the Tao and embraces softness and gentleness. He responds naturally, maintains a low profile, and acts last. In softness and stillness, he can live in balance and contentment and can overcome the greatest obstacles and wear down the hardest stone. Being soft and gentle, he does not compete with anyone. Therefore, no one can compete with him.

A powerful army will suffer an early defeat, a rigid branch will break easily, and tough leather will crack and split. The teeth may appear stronger than the tongue, but they will fall out before the tongue loses its sense of taste. Therefore, softness is the key to survival, and hardness is the cause of destruction. A sharp sword invites challenges, but who will want to challenge a dull blade? Thus, being outstanding and unique can get you into trouble, but if you maintain a low profile you will be safe.

If you rush into action, you're likely to fail. If you wait and observe before you act, you will have a better chance of succeeding. People who act rashly usually end up as guinea pigs and cannon fodder. Those who talk loud and act fast are always exposed to danger. Those who follow, however, walk on safer ground. These principles have been known for a long time, but today only a few people understand them.

Not acting does not mean preventing things from happening. Rather, it means waiting for the right moment to act. Therefore, if you understand the principles of the Tao, you can anticipate those who acted first by acting last. Timeliness is the key to everything. Act before it is appropriate, and you will fail. Act after the fact, and you will also fail. Once an opportunity is lost, it will be gone forever. It was said that King Yu did not bother to recover a hat he had lost along the way. It wasn't that he was in a hurry or that he was careless about his belongings. Rather, it was because he did not want small concerns to get in the way of important matters.

## KNOW CONTENTMENT AND LIVE SIMPLY

Live simply and find contentment, and you will preserve the energy of life. If we stray from stillness, we will leave the path of life. If we are trapped by emotions and desire, we will enter the path of death. If we abandon the formless for forms, we will be separated from the root of all things. Keep a simple agenda, and you will not feel harried. Minimize desire, and you will not have many needs. People who tax their senses will tire themselves and not be able to hear or see clearly. People who strain their mental capacity to govern will injure their hearts. Therefore, the sage achieves government through nongovernment. When the laws of the state do not deviate from the natural way, the people will not be burdened by bureaucracy and unnecessary rules and regulations.

Extreme happiness and anger are not part of the natural way. Frustration, sadness, and disharmony are the result of virtues lost. Like and dislike create illusions and upset the balance of centeredness. Pleasure and displeasure produce anxiety and disrupt the stillness of one's inner nature. Anger harms the essence of yin, and excitement injures the essence of yang. When yin and yang are unbalanced, speech will be impaired and thoughts will be scattered. When sadness and frustration accompany anger, illness is the result. If there are too many likes and dislikes, mental problems will arise.

When there is no sadness or elation, virtue can take hold. When there is no pleasure or displeasure, there is balance. To be at one with the void is to be free from desire. To be centered is to be still. To be undisturbed by worldly matters is to have mental clarity. Attain these states, and you will be united with the light of the spirit. To be united with the spirit is to have inner peace.

If you can regulate emotion and desire, you will succeed in your endeavors. If you have inner peace, you will be able to deal with the unexpected. If you are at peace with yourself, the five viscera (heart, liver, spleen, lungs, and kidneys) will be healthy, your thoughts will be clear, your tendons will be strong, and your senses will be keen. When the body is strong and the spirit is clear, you will not be frustrated by obstacles. Your actions will be neither excessive nor inadequate, and you will not be anxious and irritable when things go wrong. You will not feel constricted in a small room or disoriented in a wide-open space. Free from desire and anxiety, you will be able to live for a long time.

In ancient times people lived in caves and had few luxuries, but their spirits were strong and they were happy. Today people live like kings, but they are anxious and worried. This is because people nowadays want to rule and control instead of simply being connected to the vastness of the Tao.

People who pursue fame and power will be destroyed by their own ambition. If you spend your life accumulating wealth, you will never be happy because you will never be content. Forever trying to get what you don't have, you will eventually tire the body and harm the spirit. However, if you know the meaning of contentment, you will be able to maintain your health and live for a long time. Thus, if you value life, you must know how to distinguish between wants and needs.

You won't find true happiness living in a large and beautiful house.

You won't find it touring the world, listening to loud music, seeing glamorous shows, and tasting exquisite foods. You won't find it riding in a luxury vehicle or collecting trophies of magnificent animals. True happiness comes when you are content with what you have. If you are not excited by riches or frustrated by poverty, you are truly happy. If you are truly happy, you can be as still as yin and as brilliant as yang. When Zi Xia was a student of Confucius (551–479 B.C.E.), he admired the virtue of the sages but was also attracted to the riches. Unable to reconcile wealth and virtue, he became thin and haggard. Finally, when he understood the meaning of virtue, he regained his health.

The sage does not let the affairs of the world affect her health and well-being. She does not let desire disturb the stillness of her inner nature. She keeps her emotions in moderation between extremes and maintains her balance no matter what happens. The affairs of the world cannot occupy her thoughts because in her thoughts there is only the oneness of the Tao.

If you know the meaning of contentment, you will be comfortable sitting under a tree or sleeping in a cave. On the contrary, if you are not satisfied, you will not be happy even if you have all the treasures in the world. Only those who do not crave happiness will be truly happy, and only those who are free from elation and sadness will know true contentment. Some people are comfortable only when they are surrounded by sounds and sights. They feel happy only when there is loud music, good wine, and the company of beautiful people. However, when the party is over, they are left with an uncontrollable loneliness, as if they have lost everything.

People experience inner emptiness because they do not know the meaning of true happiness. They try to find happiness in material things and sensual pleasure, and they are sad and lonely when the music stops and the crowd leaves. Trapped in an endless cycle of elation and sadness, they do not realize that true happiness is found in stillness and inner contentment. They live out their lives in illusion, injuring themselves and losing that which can give them true happiness.

If you cannot find contentment within, you will be tempted to find satisfaction outside. But things that satisfy you externally cannot nourish your skin and strengthen your bones. Nor can they nurture your internal organs. Without inner contentment, happiness will not last even if you possess all the riches of the world.

Today many people talk about the wisdom of the ancients, but few know how to practice it. People want the wisdom but do not want the discipline required by the practices. They imitate the rituals, but their actions have no substance.

Floating leisurely on a river, riding in a luxurious carriage, watching dancers whirl around in silk, listening to music that excites, hunting water fowl by the banks of a lake, and stalking deer in the forest—these are activities that many think will bring them happiness. The sage, however, is not deluded. He knows that being attached to worldly things will weaken his spirit and disturb his inner stillness.

Living in a shack with bare walls, feeling the cold wind coming through the windows, slogging through a marsh and climbing over mountains to get provisions, being away from the comforts of a large city—these are conditions that will drive an ordinary person mad. The sage, however, does not let her surroundings affect her inner peace. The crow makes the same cries in summer and winter; why should we behave differently in good and bad times?

Life and inner nature are originally united. When the fetus emerges in the mother's womb, life is formed. When this life leaves the mother's womb, feelings of like and dislike arise. Through socialization, regulations and rules of behavior develop. However, those who have embraced the Tao do not need rules to tell them how to behave. Behaviors are only responses to situations, and if you are stuck in one mode of behavior, you will not be able to adapt to changing circumstances.

Those who can hold their inner nature of stillness are connected to the Tao. Depending on the circumstances, they can be round or square, bent or straight, bright or dull. They can change with the situation yet be as permanent as the sky and the earth. On top of a mountain, they are not tall; inside a hollow, they do not diminish in height. They are not proud when they are rich or self-conscious when they are poor. In their youth they do not dazzle; in old age they do not fade. Entering fire, they are not burned; immersed in water, they do not drown. They do not need to be powerful to be virtuous; they do not need to possess material things to be rich; they do not need to display strength to know they are strong.

Still as water, they always flow downward and follow the gentlest path. Subtle as vapor, they can rise above obstacles and float up to the sky. They hide their gold in the depths of a mountain and their pearls at

How to
detach?

Big
Picture

the bottom of the sea. Not attracted by material things and positions of power, they live out the fullness of life in contentment. Because they do not equate hardship with sadness and poverty with danger, they are not prisoners of external circumstances. Without the burdens of attachment, they are at one with the beginning and the end of things.

All creatures, even the smallest insects, are in touch with the natural way and know intuitively what is beneficial and what is harmful. They know that if they abandon their natural tendencies, they will perish. When the spirit is in command and energy is plentiful, we can distinguish colors and sounds acutely, move our limbs agilely, make observations clearly, and know the difference between true and false intuitively. When the spirit is distracted, we stumble, bump into obstacles, and have no control over our thoughts, feelings, and actions. If the spirit is occupied with little things, we are not able to see the big picture; if it is preoccupied with thoughts inside, we ignore what is happening outside; and if it is attracted to external things, we neglect internal stillness.

The body is the vehicle of life, energy is the root of life, and the spirit is the director of life. If one of them is harmed, the others will also be injured. If the body is aroused by pleasure, it will be harmed. If energy is used to drive desire, it will dissipate. If the spirit is distracted and left to wander, it will become dim.

When people do harmful things to themselves, such as walking through fire, jumping over deep crevasses, and diving into stormy seas, we consider them mad. However, we do not consider people who harm body, spirit, and energy for the sake of fame, fortune, and personal achievement insane. This is because we do not understand that striving for achievement harms body, energy, and spirit. The spirit degenerates when it is used to scheme and deceive. Energy dissipates when it is used to fuel negative emotions. The body is weakened when it is driven to achieve. When the spirit becomes too attached to worldly things, it will stray. When energy is low, it won't be able to search for the wandering spirit and lead it back to the center. When the body is weak, it will shut its doors so that the spirit cannot return. This is what happens to people who have pushed their mental activity beyond limits and worked their bodies to exhaustion.

# 2

# The Nature of Reality

## WHAT IS REAL?

When we dream, we don't know we are dreaming. When we dream we are a bird, we sense that we are flying. When we dream we are a fish, we sense that we are swimming in the waters. Dreams feel real. It is only upon waking up that we realize we have dreamed.

There was once a man who was transformed into a tiger. When his brother came to see him, the man, who was now a tiger, mauled him. We cannot say that this man lost his senses and killed his brother, because when this man became a tiger, the other man was no longer his brother. When he was a tiger, he had no idea what it was like to be human, and when he was human, he could not imagine what it was like to be a tiger.

We assume that the reality that we live in is the ultimate reality. While we are experiencing this reality, we cannot conceive of other realities. However, when we transcend this reality, we realize that we have been dreaming, and after awakening from the dream, we cannot imagine how we could have lived in illusion and not known it.

In winter, water freezes and becomes ice; in summer, ice melts and becomes water. We accept these facts because we know that this is the natural way of things. However, when things turn from good to bad, we fret. This is because we do not understand that good and bad times are also part of the natural way of things.

If the body is exposed to extreme heat, cold, dryness, and dampness, it will be injured. Injure the body, and the spirit will be harmed. If the spirit is affected by excitement, elation, sadness, frustration, and worry, it will be weakened. Weaken the spirit, and the body will be injured. We are alive because spirit and body are together. If they are separated, we will die. Planning and scheming dissipate the spirit; hard labor drains the body of vigor. If the energy of either body or spirit is spent, the two will separate and we will die.

When an old horse dies, its skin withers and its hide becomes brittle. However, the fur of a dead puppy is soft and warm. This is because one animal has used up its life energy and the other has not. When a young person dies an unnatural death, the energy lingers even though the body is dead. This energy can become a ghost to haunt the realm of the living. When an old person dies naturally after living a long life, all the energy is spent. The dead person's soul will therefore rest in peace. Knowing this, we should care for our bodies and spirits and allow our energy to run its natural course. In this way, we can live in contentment and die in peace.

The Tao is the underlying reality of all things. It can smooth the rugged and straighten the crooked. Therefore, if you are connected with the Tao, you will not be hindered by obstacles. Embrace the Tao, and you will be able to come to terms with both good and bad times. If you choose to be a leader, your skills will be respected and you will be honored; if you choose to be a hermit, you will enjoy happiness and contentment.

It is usually after a winter storm that we appreciate the ability of evergreen trees to weather the cold. Similarly, it is during times of hardship and danger that we appreciate the ability of the sage to hold on to the Tao and not forget its principles. Only those who can embrace the sky can cover the earth. Only those who embody the great clarity can see things as they are without preconceptions. And only those who have the courage to walk in darkness can be as bright as the sun and the moon.

Use the Tao as a rod, virtue as the line, propriety and music as the hook, and compassion and integrity as the bait. Cast them into the river or drop them into the ocean, and all the things in the world will come to you.

The Tao is at the origin of things. It penetrates the sky and the earth and extends beyond the four directions. It lets things be and does not control or manipulate them. If we understand the workings of the Tao, we will not try to change the natural way of things. We will know that if things are left to themselves, they will be in harmony with the Tao. This is not because the Tao has made them so but because the Tao lets them run their course.

## THE ENLIGHTENED PERSON

Enlightened people can influence others by their presence. In their company, the poor will not feel dejected, the rich and powerful will not feel privileged, and the brave will not be proud. Teachers will not need to teach, and ministers will not need to advise. Guided by nonaction, the sage does not need to speak to inspire others. Like a dragon or a snake, he can lengthen or shorten, expand or contract, and move or rest according to the demands of the situation. Externally, his behavior is consonant with the times; internally he keeps his own principles. His actions do not dazzle, his eyes and ears do not judge, and his thoughts do not wander. United with the spirit, he embraces simplicity and lives in the realm of the great clarity. Because he is in harmony with all things, everything blooms in his presence.

The enlightened person knows that the sky, the earth, the four directions, the breath of yin and yang, the moisture of rain and dew, and acts of virtue are all part of the greater scheme of things belonging to a universal harmonious order. There are many species of trees, but they are all the same in the eyes of the Tao. Different nations have different customs, but to the Tao they are one large family of people. Everything in the universe is connected. It is said that seeing the flight of ravens and hearing the sound of flutes can conjure images of the frontier. When clouds gather, rain will fall. When moisture penetrates the earth, it becomes one with the soil. Cloud, rain, water, and soil respond to one another not because they have certain skills but because they are part of the natural way of things. Focus on differences, and things in proximity will feel distant. Focus on unity, and everything will be connected and related to everything else.

Many philosophers try to solve the problems of the world, but they can only offer limited solutions. This is because they are not connected with the Source. For example, Sunzi (544–496 B.C.E.), Mozi (470–391 B.C.E.), and Mencius (372–289 B.C.E.) all had different views on good government and effective leadership, but their teachings are like single spokes on a wheel that are neither necessary nor sufficient for the wheel to function. Although it is possible to build a functioning wheel without spokes, it is not possible to build a wheel with only spokes. It is the structural roundness of the wheel, not the spokes, that makes the wheel work.

The sage knows that when something is separated from its source, its use is limited. Take, for example, the bits of metal that fly from the forge when a sword is being hammered on the anvil. These metal bits do not have much use in and of themselves because they are not part of the sword being made at the forge. They may have small uses, but because they are disconnected from the larger whole, they cannot be made into a functional object. Therefore, things that are not connected to the greater order cannot be the touchstone of reality, and teachings that are not connected to the Tao cannot offer a vision of the greater order of things.

Today, people are more concerned with acquiring skill than being connected to the natural way. Martial artists, calligraphers, and even government ministers all learn from a standard set of instructions. If these disciplines are learned separately, a skilled calligrapher cannot become an accomplished warrior, and an expert martial artist cannot become a good minister. Skill is specific to a single area of expertise and does not give us an understanding of the nature of action. If you understand the natural way, however, you will know that the principles behind calligraphy, the martial arts, and statecraft are the same.

When something is removed from the Source, it no longer has the same properties. Cloth dyed black can appear darker than the dye, but the dyed cloth cannot be used as the source of the dye. Similarly, knowledge is diluted when it is removed from the Source. The farther it is from the Source, the less effective it will be. Even the teachings recorded in books are empty words if they are not connected to the Source.

If the sky is not balanced, the sun and the moon will not follow their paths. If the earth is not balanced, trees and grass will not grow. If we are not in harmony and at peace with ourselves, we will not be able to distinguish truth from lies. Therefore, true knowledge can only come from the heart of an enlightened person. If we do not know the ultimate reality, how can we know whether something is true or false?

The sage puts her spirit at the center of her being and returns to the state before things were born, but she is able to see, hear, and act in clarity. Because she has no intention, she can accomplish great things. Because she knows through not-knowing, she can understand the ultimate reality.

To be kind, compassionate, and generous and to bring happiness to others—this is benevolence. Achieving great deeds, commanding respect from others, setting things in order, separating private and public interests, discriminating the useful from the useless, keeping the country safe, training others for succession, putting down rebellions, building temples and shrines, and being kind to orphans and widows—this is integrity. Closing the nine openings of the body, hiding intention and will, abandoning know-how, returning to the state of not-knowing, wandering far from the dust of the world, living leisurely in the realm of nonaction, embracing yin and yang, and being at one with everything—this is virtue.

## THE TAO AND VIRTUE

When the Tao flourishes, there is virtue. When virtue is absent, benevolence and integrity emerge. Once benevolence and integrity are here to stay, virtue will be gone. Laozi (604–531 B.C.E.) once said that the great Tao can dissolve benevolence and integrity and that benevolence and integrity can destroy the Tao. This is because when there is virtue, there is no need for benevolence and integrity. When virtue is gone, benevolence and integrity are needed to maintain order in society. Virtue is part of the Tao; benevolence and integrity are creations of humanity. Virtue is part of the natural way; benevolence and integrity appear when the natural way is abandoned.

When society disintegrates, philosophers and teachers appear. In the final years of the Zhou Dynasty (1046–256 B.C.E.), the followers of Confucius and Mozi debated what the best form of government is and how to end social strife. They promoted their ideas and attacked their opponents. If they could not impress people with flowery speeches, they intimidated them with a display of knowledge. They posed as champions of social harmony and promoted culture and rules of behavior. Complicating an already complex society, codes of correct actions multiplied. People began to accept the expectations set up by society. They wanted to realize their ambitions, leave a visible legacy of their accomplishments, and be admired by future generations. They displayed their virtue, promoted their abilities, and abandoned the real for the false. As a result, they became ill and weak as they strayed farther and farther from the path of life.

## THE SAGE AND VIRTUE

The sage is never far from virtue, and virtue is never far from the Tao.

When a large and beautiful tree is felled, it becomes just like any other tree. Floating down the river, it may appear better than logs of lower quality, but the essential difference between it and the other trees is gone. This is because it lost its essence when it was removed from the earth. Similarly, a person who loses his or her essence becomes an empty hulk. When spirit and energy stray, words and promises are empty. When virtue departs, actions are insincere. When the connection with the Tao is broken, behaviors are dictated by external pressure. Without essence, a person is an empty shell, acting to please others rather than following his or her own true nature. Smothered by desire and greed, he or she is no longer rooted in the Origin. Buried in the dust of the world, he or she becomes a slave of desire and a prisoner of the will of others.

The sage focuses on his inner nature and is not concerned with external form and appearances. Not allowing worldly matters to distract his senses, he can journey to the realm of clarity, know the depth of the springs of the earth, and explore the nine levels of the sky. He can merge with the realm of the void and wander in the expanse of nothingness. Externally, he can travel beyond this world; internally, he can rest within the abode of his spirit. With the wind and rain as heralds and the stars as companions, he can travel far and wide, for there is nothing in the universe that can bind or hold him.

The sage returns her inner nature to its beginnings and guides her spirit to the realm of the void. She follows the supreme teachings of the limitless and lives in a state of complete emptiness. The ordinary person, however, lives in a world consisting of rules and regulations that are designed to constrain her inner nature. Her thoughts are filled with anxiety, and her senses are fatigued by constant excitement. She promotes pettiness in the name of benevolence, integrity, and culture so that she can display her skills and gain fame and recognition.

The void is the home of the Tao, and simplicity is its nature. When we tax spirit and energy to gain fame and fortune, we will stray from the abode of the spirit and lose our clarity. The ordinary person wants what he does not have. People who don't like the cold will long for the heat of the summer; those who can't stand the heat will want the cool breezes of autumn. The poor want to be rich, the rich want to be famous, and the famous want to have power. The sage, however, is free from the burdens and desires of the ordinary person because he is in touch with the greater order of things.

Carp is found in deep river gorges and not in a puddle of water on a muddy road. Large trees are found on high mountains and not in a small backyard. Similarly, the greatness of the Tao is found in the bright spirit of the sage and not in the limited consciousness of the ordinary person.

If I had to choose between having friends and possessing the world, I would choose to have friends. If I had to choose between being liked by others and being at one with the beginning and end of things, I would choose to be at one with the beginning and end of things, to wander between existence and nonexistence.

The sage is in touch with the nature of things. In summer, she does not wear a coat. In winter, she does not carry a fan. She cooks according to her appetite and buys clothing according to her needs. If you are content with the essentials, how can desire creep into your life? Those who truly own the world do not pursue ambitions, and those who are truly honored do not seek fame. Those who want to be recognized, however, display virtuous behavior and hope that their actions will win praise and respect. They do not know that virtuous behaviors are but appearances and that to try to return to the Origin through appearances is as difficult as trying to get roots to grow from leaves.

The sage does not feel elated when he is praised or dejected when he is blamed. At peace with life and death, he is not excited about living or anxious about dying. Even if he is engulfed by fire or swept by floods, his spirit remains calm and balanced.

It is natural for water to be clear and still; it is the presence of mud that makes it murky. Human nature tends toward stillness; it is desire that makes it attached to things. The ear responds to sound, the eye to light, the tongue to taste, the nose to smell, and the skin to heat and cold. However, when there is desire, the eyes see beauty and ugliness, and the ears hear praise and criticism. When the senses respond to likes and dislikes, they lose their natural function. As a result, we will not be able to see a pit in our path or hear the thunder of an approaching storm.

The spirit is the well of intelligence. If its source is clear, intelligence will be clear. If intelligence is bright, the heart will be peaceful. Troubled waters cannot produce clear reflections, but the surface of calm waters will image everything clearly. A rusty plate is not an effective mirror, but a piece of polished metal will produce a clear image. Similarly, true nature is revealed most clearly when the thoughts are still. If the Tao grows in your heart, peace and contentment will follow. Just as a polished mirror is not tainted by dust, a clear intelligence is not distracted by desire and craving.

The spirit is the root, and intelligence is its branches. If we try to recover the root by gathering the branches, we will never get to the Source. However, if we can hold on to the roots, the branches will naturally be gathered.

When the eye is busy scrutinizing a piece of hair, the ear will not hear the sound of distant thunder. When the ear is busy discriminating minute differences in musical tones, the eye will not notice distant mountains. When we are too concerned with details, we will not see the big picture of things. Similarly, when we are attracted to things in the world, it is difficult to hold on to the great Tao and keep the stillness within.

Muddy water becomes clear only after it has been left undisturbed for a long time. However, clear water will become murky the moment mud is thrown into it. Similarly, although it takes time and discipline to dissolve your thoughts, it takes only one speck of desire to disrupt the stillness.

## FOLLOWING THE NATURAL WAY

Following the natural way brings harmony and prosperity. When the ways of the Tao were followed, merchants prospered, farmers reaped good harvests, and hermits were free to cultivate the Tao. Even civil servants were diligent in their duties. During those times, wind and rain did not destroy houses, grass and trees did not wither, the nine regions of the country stood firm, jade stones and pearls were large and bright, and the sages were able to use their wisdom to benefit others. Things went well for everyone because the sagely rulers followed the way of their ancestors and placed the welfare of the people above all other concerns.

When the ways of the Tao were abandoned, things went badly for everyone. Honest citizens were imprisoned and tortured, farmers lost their crops, merchants could not do business, earthquakes and floods devastated the country, people and animals were born deformed, and sages were nowhere to be found.

When a lake dries up, the fish disappear. When a forest is stripped of trees, the birds vanish. When the ways of the Tao are abandoned, the sages hide. Like fish and birds, sages need a conducive environment in which to flourish. This is why things are better for everyone if the ways of the Tao are followed.

Prosperous cities can be reduced to rubble overnight by an earthquake. When natural disasters strike, everyone is affected: rich and poor, sage and criminal, coward and warrior. When fire sweeps through a forest, everything is burned: trees, flowers, weeds, medicinal herbs, and poisonous plants. Fish and marine life cannot thrive in polluted waters; fruits and grains are damaged if there is an early frost. Similarly, the sage will not thrive if the environment does not support her existence.

A horse tied to a fence is no different from a mule; we can appreciate the speed of the horse only if it is given the freedom to run. A monkey in a cage is no different from a chicken; we can appreciate the monkey's cunning only if it is allowed to explore. When King Shun was a farmer and a blacksmith, he could only help his neighbors. However, when he became emperor, he was able to help all the people in his kingdom. This is not because he was more virtuous as a king than as a farmer, but because as a leader he had more opportunities to exercise his virtue.

When conditions are right, things will thrive; when conditions are not conducive, things will wither. Thus, when life is nurtured by the stillness of inner nature, it will flourish; when inner nature is nourished by the fullness of life, it will develop; and when people are born and raised in times of peace and harmony, they will naturally become sages.

# 3

# The Natural World

## IN THE BEGINNING

Before sky and earth were separated, everything was formless and un-differentiated. This was called the Great Beginning. The Great Beginning gave birth to the void, and the void gave birth to the universe. In the universe was vapor, and when vapor became differentiated, it separated into sky and earth. The clear light vapor of yang rose to become the sky, and the heavy muddy vapor of yin sank to become the earth. Since the vapor of yang rose faster than the vapor of yin could sink, the sky was formed before the earth.

When the primordial energies of the earth and the sky copulated, yin and yang emerged. The interaction of yin and yang generated the four seasons, and the cycles of the four seasons gave life to all things. The essence of yang was gathered to form fire, and from the essence of fire the sun was born. The essence of yin was gathered to form water, and from the essence of water the moon was born. When the procreative essences of the sun and moon were brought together, the stars emerged.

## THE WAYS OF NATURE

The sky is round; the earth is square. Squareness is associated with darkness, and roundness is associated with brightness. Brightness expands and spreads outward; therefore, it is manifested in the rays of the sun. Darkness contains and draws inward; therefore, it is manifested in the light of the moon. That which expands initiates the beginning of things, and that which contains completes the transformation.

When the expansive vapor of the sky is angry, there is wind. When the containing vapor of the earth is harmonious, there is rain. When the vapors of yin and yang compete, there is thunder; when they are unruly, there is fog. If yang dominates yin, the fog becomes rain or dew; if yin dominates yang, the fog becomes frost or snow.

Creatures with fur and feathers are yang in nature. Therefore, it is natural for them to run and fly. Creatures with scales and shells are yin in nature. Therefore, it is natural for them to hide. The sun contains the essence of yang. Yang-oriented animals respond to the sun by shedding their fur and plumage in summer and thickening them in winter. The moon contains the essence of yin. When the moon wanes, fish diminish in size and the bodies of mollusks shrink.

Fire rises and water descends. Therefore, birds, which are yang in nature, fly in the sky, and fish, which are yin in nature, dive to the bottom of the sea.

All things are connected and respond to one another. When the tiger roars, wind will whistle through the valleys. When the dragon flies, clouds will be formed in the sky. When lions fight, there will be eclipses of the sun and the moon. When whales die, shooting stars will appear. When silkworms spin their cocoons, the strings of the zither will become brittle and break. When the planet Venus falls to the horizon, the waters of the sea will become restless.

The actions of humanity also affect the natural world. When there is lot of killing, gales and tornadoes will appear. When power is misused, locusts and other harmful insects will multiply. When innocent people are killed, there will be drought. When there is injustice, there will be floods and rainstorms. Therefore, spring, summer, autumn, and winter are enforcers of celestial judgment. The sun and the moon are celestial messengers, the conjunction of stars and planets signifies a gathering of celestial power, and rainbows and shooting stars are omens.

## THE SKY AND THE EARTH

There are nine domains in the celestial realm, arranged in a grid of nine squares. The square in the center, called the central celestial domain, is the highest part of the celestial realm.

There are five "roving stars" (planets). The metal star rules the west. Its animal is the white tiger, and it is associated with autumn and the color white. The wood star rules the east. Its animal is the green dragon, and it is associated with spring and the color green. The water star rules the north. Its animal is the black tortoise, and it is associated with winter and the color black. The fire star rules the south. Its animal is the red raven (or phoenix), and it is associated with summer and the color red. The earth star rules the center. Its animal is the yellow dragon, and it is associated with all four seasons and the color yellow.

The earth lies within the six realms (north, south, east, west, above, and below) and the four directions, which are delineated by the apparent paths of the sun, the moon, and the stars. Each year is ruled by a guardian star and regulated by the four seasons.

Land extending east and west is measured by longitude, and land extending north and south is measured by latitude. Mountains are associated with benevolence and virtue; they are the root of all things. Water is associated with intelligence and judgment; it rewards and punishes. High ground is yang; therefore, it is associated with activity. Low ground is yin; therefore, it is associated with rest. Mounds are yang and male in nature. Hollows are yin and female in nature.

## THE SEASONS

The eight winds mark eight seasonal changes. Approximately forty-five days after the winter solstice, the *slanting-rain wind* arrives. In ancient times, this is when prisoners who committed petty crimes were released. Approximately forty-five days later, the *cleansing and forgiving wind* arrives. During this time, the fields are inspected and irrigation ditches are repaired. Approximately forty-five days later, the *bright and clear wind* arrives. At this time the people offer their best woven cloth to the sky in thanksgiving. Approximately forty-five days later, the *goodwill wind* arrives. This is when common citizens who have contributed to the welfare of the state are rewarded. Approximately forty-five days later, the *cool-breeze wind* arrives. At this time grains and fruits are offered to the earth in thanksgiving. Approximately forty-five days later, the *confining wind* arrives. During this time, musical instruments are packed and stored. Approximately forty-five days later, the *noncirculating wind* arrives. This is the time when houses, public buildings, and roads are repaired. Approximately forty-five days later, the *frontier wind* arrives. At this time, the city gates are closed and the bridges are drawn. It is also the time when certain types of criminals are punished.

## THE FIVE ELEMENTS

Wood chokes earth, earth blocks water, water extinguishes fire, fire destroys metal, and metal cuts wood. Rice grows in spring and dies in autumn, peppers grow in summer and die in winter, wheat grows in autumn and dies in summer, and legumes and root vegetables grow in winter and die in summer.

When wood is strong, water is weak. When fire begins to strengthen, metal suffocates and earth dies. When fire is strong, wood is weak. When earth begins to strengthen, water suffocates and metal dies. When earth is strong, fire is weak. When metal begins to strengthen, wood suffocates and water dies. When metal is strong, earth is weak. When water begins to strengthen, fire suffocates and wood dies. When water is strong, metal is weak. When wood begins to strengthen, earth suffocates and fire dies.

There are five primary colors, five flavors, and five elements. Of the colors—yellow, white, black, green, and red—yellow is dominant. Of the five flavors—sweet, spicy, sour, salty, and bitter—sweet is dominant. Of the five elements—metal, wood, water, fire, and earth—earth is dominant.

Strengthen wood to restrain earth, cultivate wood to strengthen fire, restrain fire to strengthen clouds, cultivate clouds to obtain rain (water), and strengthen earth to restrain water. Use earth to neutralize water, use water to overcome fire, use fire to melt metal, and use metal to restrain wood. These are the principles of the interactions of the five elements.

## THE NATURAL CYCLE OF THE SEASONS AND THE MONTHS

The ancient sages were in tune with the seasons. They observed the changes in nature and kept in touch with the natural order of things. If humanity is not in harmony with the seasons, the balance of nature will be disrupted and disasters will occur.

The first solar month is at the beginning of spring. The ceremonies

## Table 1. Solar months with corresponding wind seasons and activities

| Month | Month name | Season marker | Western date | Wind | Activity |
|---|---|---|---|---|---|
| 1 | yin | first day of spring[*] | Feb. 4 | slanting-rain wind | releasing petty criminals |
| | | coming of rains | Feb. 19 | | |
| 2 | mao | insects awaken | Mar. 6 | | |
| | | spring equinox | Mar. 20 | cleansing and forgiving wind | digging and repairing irrigation ditches |
| 3 | chen | bright and clear | Apr. 5 | | |
| | | rains for growth | Apr. 20 | | |
| 4 | si | first day of summer | May 6 | bright and clear wind | offering cloth to the sky |
| | | stalks appear | May 21 | | |
| 5 | wu | grains on stalks | June 6 | | |
| | | summer solstice | June 20 | goodwill wind | rewarding those who help the community |
| 6 | wei | lesser heat | July 7 | | |
| | | greater heat | July 20 | | |
| 7 | shen | first day of autumn | Aug. 8 | cool-breeze wind | offering grains and fruits to the earth |
| | | end of heat | Aug. 23 | | |
| 8 | yu | dew turns white | Sept. 8 | | |
| | | autumn equinox | Sept. 22 | confining wind | packing away musical instruments |
| 9 | xu | cold dew | Oct. 8 | | |
| | | coming of frost | Oct. 23 | | |
| 10 | hai | first day of winter | Nov. 8 | noncirculating wind | repairing buildings and roads |
| | | light snow | Nov. 21 | | |
| 11 | zi | heavy snow | Dec. 7 | | |
| | | winter solstice | Dec. 21 | frontier wind | closing city gates |
| 12 | chou | light freeze | Jan. 6 | | |
| | | deep freeze | Jan. 20 | | |

* In the Chinese calendar, the first day of spring is not the spring equinox, as the Western calendar assigns, nor is the autumn equinox the first day of autumn; instead, the equinoxes mark the midpoint of the seasons. The same distinction applies for the summer and winter solstices.

in this month focus on blessing the household. When the east winds begin to blow, the ice melts. The worms stir, the fish swim to the surface of the lakes, the bears awaken from hibernation and hunt fish at the river shallows, and the ravens begin their journey north.

In this month, the enlightened ruler rewards trustworthy subjects, lessens the burdens of the people, and reduces taxes. On the first day of spring, the priests purify the ceremonial grounds, offer jade to the spirits, and ask for blessings and protection. Logging is forbidden, as are the gathering of eggs and the hunting of female animals. In this month, there is no construction of government and public buildings, because the people need to recover from a long winter.

If the appropriate ceremonies for the month are not performed, there will be disasters. If the rites of summer are performed in spring, wind and rain will be unpredictable, grass and trees will wither, and there will be fear and anxiety among the people. If the rites of autumn are performed in spring, there will be epidemics, tornadoes, and rainstorms. Weeds will also grow out of control and destroy the crops. If the rites of winter are performed in spring, floods, hailstorms, and early frost will destroy the harvest.

The second month is in the middle of spring. Soft rains begin to fall, and the prune and cherry trees start to flower. Worms and insects emerge from their nests and holes. The sound of the yellow birds is heard, and hawks and eagles are seen hovering over the fields.

In this month, the judges inspect the prisons and lessen the sentences of offenders who have committed lesser crimes. Wardens are reminded to treat the prisoners fairly; gifts are sent to orphans, widows, and the elderly; and attention is given to the cultivation of roots and tubers.

During this month, the weighing scales of merchants are inspected to ensure that they comply with government standards. Opening the gates of irrigation ditches, burning trees, and using nets to catch fish are all prohibited. There are no military excursions or training this month because the citizens need to get their fields plowed.

If the rites of autumn are performed in the second month, there will be floods, icy winds, and violent crimes. If the rites of winter are performed, the breath of yang will not be sufficient to withstand the cold air. Consequently, the wheat crop will be destroyed, and there will be famine and social disorder. If the rites of summer are performed, there will be drought. The heat waves will arrive early, and insects will ruin the crops.

The third month is at the end of spring. In this month, trees begin to bloom, and field mice can be seen scampering in the fields. Rainbows are frequent, and water lilies begin to grow in the ponds.

During this month, boats are inspected and damages are repaired. Fish is offered at the shrines, and special ceremonies are performed to ensure a good harvest at sea. The breath of life is strongest in the third month because the vapor of yang penetrates deep into the earth to make all things grow. Farmers are encouraged to devote all their efforts to cultivation. No tribute is collected, and poor families are given subsidies of seeds and farming supplies. Gifts of cloth and coins are sent to the nobles and civil servants who have contributed to the welfare of the state. Dams and irrigation ditches are inspected and repaired before the start of the rainy season. To prevent flooding, each town mobilizes its citizens to repair the dikes and dredge the water channels. The sale and transportation of hunting weapons, poison, and traps are forbidden, as is the cutting of mulberry trees.

In this month, the forest is alive with birds, the leaves of the mulberry tree are fully grown, and the equipment for silk making is readied. The emperor's courtiers are instructed to abstain from meat, take ritual baths, and help with the gathering of silk. The government's storage of gold, iron, leather, and dyes are inspected, and silk- and clothing-making equipment is upgraded or repaired. Special days are set aside for fairs and festivities so that the people can rest and enjoy music and entertainment. At the fairs, stud animals from the imperial stables are made available for breeding so that farmers and herders can maintain a healthy stock of oxen and horses. Throughout the country, ceremonial offerings are made at the city gates to ward off evil and destructive forces.

If the rituals for this month are performed correctly, there will be adequate rain in the growing season. However, if the rites of winter are performed in this month, there will be cold winds in the growing season. Crops will die, and there will be fear and anxiety among the people. If the rites of summer are performed, there will be epidemics. Rain will be inadequate, and the trees and grass will die. If the rites of autumn are performed, the sky will be cloudy, and there will be floods, war, and destruction.

The fourth month is at the beginning of summer. The ceremonies of this month focus on honoring the spirit of the hearth. With the coming of summer, the sounds of crickets and toads are heard. Night crawlers emerge from the tilled earth, the peach trees bear fruit, and bitter melons ripen.

On the first day of summer, ceremonies welcoming the summer are performed south of the capital. After the ceremony, government officials who have contributed to the welfare of the state are promoted. A feast is prepared, and citizens known for their virtue and filial piety are recruited into the civil service.

During this month, no buildings are to be demolished, no new structures erected, and no large trees felled. Grasslands are inspected, and their natural resources are estimated. Farmers are told to watch for wild animals and birds that may destroy the crops. When the first grains of the wheat are harvested, there are ceremonies of thanksgiving, and petty criminals are released from prison.* In this month, the state apothecaries are inspected to ensure that there are sufficient herbs in case of epidemics.

If the rites of autumn are performed in early summer, there will be excessive rain, and crops will not grow. People in the villages will starve, and the cities will be filled with beggars. If the rites of winter are performed, grass and trees will wither early, and cities will be destroyed by floods. If the rites of spring are performed, there will be locusts and windstorms, and the fruits will not ripen.

The fifth month is in the middle of summer. At this time, yang is at its height. Praying mantises are seen in the fields, bird songs are heard in the woods, and the sounds of the toads have disappeared. The ceremonies of this month focus on honoring the spirits of the mountains, rivers, and springs. During this month, the important ceremony of rainmaking is also performed. The rituals are accompanied by music and the offering of wheat grains, chickens, apricots, and peaches.

In this month, the cutting of blue grass and the burning of charcoal for cloth dying are forbidden, as is the drying of large quantities of cloth under the hot sun. The city gates are opened, and merchandise from the

---

* The *Spring and Autumn Annals,* a Chinese historical text compiled in the fifth century B.C.E., states that petty criminals were released at this time so that they could help farm.

border towns is made available in the markets. The sentences of serious offenders are reduced, and food and supplies are given to widows, orphans, and the elderly.

During this month, the oxen and the horses are pregnant. Livestock is rounded up, horses are trained, and the pregnant animals are put in separate stalls for safety.

As summer reaches its height, the deer grow their antlers, the sounds of cicadas are heard, and the summer grasses are tall. Open fires in the countryside are prohibited. Shepherds are encouraged to take their flocks to high pastures, and citizens are allowed to move to the mountains or live in tree houses to escape the heat.

If the rites of winter are performed in the fifth month, hail and frost will damage the crops, roads will be blocked by landslides, and there will be mutiny among the troops. If the rites of spring are performed, the crops will not ripen, harmful insects will destroy the seeds, and there will be famine. If the rites of autumn are performed, grass and trees will wither, fruits will be sour, and there will be drought and plagues.

After the summer solstice, the breath of yin begins to rise. Yang and yin vie for control, and as the breath of yin continues to grow, life gives way to decay and death. During this time, people need to purify themselves by abstaining from meat and sensual activities. Government ministers and officials should use this time to observe the changes of yin and yang and plan their policies.

The sixth month is at the end of summer. During this month, the cool winds begin to blow. Crickets hide in the cracks in the walls, young eagles take their first flight, and the grass is cut for fodder. The ceremonies of this month focus on honoring the guardians of the earth and the four directions.

In this month, the fishermen are mobilized to capture sea snakes and sharks so that the waters are safe for travel. Woodlands are inspected, and fodder is collected and stored. The dead are remembered in memorial services, the sick are comforted, and the elderly are given supplies of rice. The newly dead are buried with gifts and offerings so that they can make their journey back to the earth.

By the end of summer, the trees are at the height of their growth. The logging of growing trees is prohibited; only dead trees and fallen branches are allowed to be gathered for firewood. The soil is moist and rich, the weather is hot, and there is frequent rain. This is when the grass should be cut and mulched, so that the soil will be rich for the years to come. In this month, there is no large-scale public construction and no conscription.

If the rites of spring are performed in late summer, the grains will wither. The people will suffer from colds and respiratory diseases, and there will be many homeless people wandering the countryside. If the rites of autumn are performed, there will be floods in the lowlands. Crops will not ripen, and there will be birth defects and infant mortality. If the rites of winter are performed, cold winds will blow. Vultures will prey on young animals, and the people will abandon their fields to take shelter in the cities.

The seventh month is at the beginning of autumn. The ceremonies of the seventh month focus on honoring the guardians of doors and entrances. In this month, cool winds blow and frost begins to fall. The sounds of the winter cicadas are heard, and eagles and hawks increase their hunting activity. This is also the time when prisoners on death row are executed.

During this month, citizens who are unfilial, disrespectful, and quarrelsome are brought before the magistrates and punished. On the first day of autumn, the ceremony of welcoming the season is performed in the fields west of the capital. After the ceremony, military officers and soldiers who have demonstrated bravery are rewarded. The commanders are instructed to train the troops and raise morale. Soldiers who have distinguished themselves in training are promoted and given the chance to lead military excursions against bandits and insubordinate tribute kingdoms. Patrols are increased along the nation's borders to ensure that the frontier towns are protected from invasion. In the towns and villages, the judges review the codes of law, inspect the prisons, and try cases of rape and domestic violence.

In the beginning of autumn, things in the natural world begin to decay. The last grains are harvested, taxes are collected, dams are strengthened, government buildings are repaired, and public construction projects are initiated. In this month, no titles are invested, no ambassadors are sent, and no coins are minted.

If the rites of this month are performed properly, the heat of summer will dissipate and the cool winds will arrive. However, if the rites of winter are performed in autumn, the breath of yin will stifle the land.

Insects will destroy the harvest, and there will be war. If the rites of spring are performed, there will be drought. The breath of yang will choke the land, and the five grains will not ripen. If the rites of summer are performed, there will be forest fires in winter. Heat and cold will be unpredictable, and there will be epidemics.

The eighth month is at the height (middle) of autumn. At this time, flocks of migrating birds are seen heading for warmer lands.

During this month, serious offenders and hardened criminals are sentenced. Prison security is increased, and justice is carried out swiftly. The elderly are given clothing and food supplies. Military installations, barracks, bridges, irrigation ditches, granaries, barns, and warehouses are repaired or built. Grain, dried vegetables, and hay are collected into warehouses in preparation for winter. Farmers are encouraged to plant wheat before winter arrives, and those who neglect their duties are fined.

In midautumn, the breath of life continues to dissipate. The vapor of yang decreases daily. Water begins to chill. At this time of year, weights and measures are checked and calibrated. Border gates are unlocked, markets are opened, and merchants are encouraged to travel between villages. Goods from different parts of the country are circulated and sold, citizens are encouraged to travel for leisure, and people from foreign countries are invited to visit and conduct business. In this way, the economy of the nation thrives, and the treasury is filled.

If the rites of spring are performed at the height of autumn, there will be no rain. Flowers and trees will not wither, to prepare for winter, and there will be fear and distrust among the people. If the rites of summer are performed, there will be severe drought. The worms will not burrow into the earth, and there will be no harvest the next year. If the rites of winter are performed, there will be windstorms and untimely rain, and grass and trees will wither early.

The ninth month is at the end of autumn. By this time, the birds have migrated south. The chrysanthemum flowers are in bloom, and leopards and tigers are constantly hunting.

During this month, frost begins to fall. Dried food, fodder, firewood, and other provisions are collected and stored for the winter. Public works are halted. Construction workers and farmers are advised to return home so that they will not be exposed to the chilly winds. The rate of taxation and tribute for the next year, based on the yield of the past year, is announced.

In the last month of autumn, soldiers are drilled and assigned to battalions. Commanders, troops, and war machines are assembled in the training fields, and military exercises are conducted.

By this time of year, the grass has withered, the trees are without leaves, and animals have burrowed into the ground. The cutting of trees is prohibited; firewood must be gathered from fallen branches. Criminal cases are tried, and sentences are passed. Delinquent taxes and tribute are collected, and excesses are returned. Obstacles are cleared from the roads to ensure that traffic on the main thoroughfares can move smoothly.

If the rites of summer are performed in late autumn, there will be disastrous flooding. The provisions stored for winter will be damaged, and there will be widespread epidemics of colds and respiratory problems. If the rites of winter are performed, bandits and thieves will thrive. Border towns will be invaded, and there will be earthquakes. If the rites of spring are performed, there will be hot winds in the cool months. The people will be lazy and weak, and there will be war and violence.

The tenth month is at the beginning of winter. The ceremonies of this month focus on honoring the spirit of wells and springs.

In this month, water begins to freeze. The ground is cold, and earthworms have disappeared. The nation is readied for winter. The relocation of homes is prohibited, and those caught on the road are transported back to their respective hometowns. Criminals on death row are executed, and instigators of civil disturbance are punished.

On the first day of winter, the ceremony of welcoming the winter season is performed in the fields north of the capital. After the ceremony, those who have died in the service of the nation are honored. Gifts are sent to their families and descendants, and orphans and widows are comforted. The breath of yin reaches its height on this day.

During this month, all the grains are gathered into granaries. The city walls are inspected and repaired, guards are posted at the gates, and the locks on the gates are secured. The border patrols are put on alert, and roads and footpaths along the frontier are cleared of obstacles.

At this time of year, the funeral rites are reviewed, and the work of engravers and casket makers is inspected. If the work is below standard, the craftspeople are punished.

In this month, feasts and offerings are made to the Earth Mother, the ancestors, and the celestial lords in thanks for a prosperous year.

Farmers are rewarded, military commanders are tested, and taxes are collected from those who harvest fish and kelp. However, since this is winter, the taxes are minimal.

If the rites of spring are performed in early winter, water will not freeze. The vapors of the earth will rise, and people will be forced out of their homes. If the rites of summer are performed, there will be strong warm winds, and swarms of insects will appear. If the rites of autumn are performed, frost and snow will be untimely. There will be disturbances and skirmishes along the border, and land will be lost to invaders.

The eleventh month is in the middle of winter. At this time, the ice on the lakes thickens, the ground is covered with snow, the birds are silent, and tigers and other large animals begin to choose their mates.

This is a time of rest. There is no public construction, no building of new houses, and no mobilization of workforces. The soil must not be disturbed in midwinter. Otherwise, hibernating animals will die, and there will be epidemics. The police are instructed to increase their vigilance. Robbers, thieves, and rapists who are arrested are punished immediately.

During this month, wine is brewed. The wine containers are cleaned, the ingredients are measured, and the brewers are told to use the best millet and rice and the purest water. Offerings are made to the oceans, the rivers, and the great lakes. Grains and animals abandoned in the open fields are free for the taking. The wardens of the forests and marshes announce that hunting and the gathering of wild edible plants are permitted. However, disputes over game and foraged foods are not tolerated, and offenders are punished and fined.

In midwinter, the ruler and the ministers are encouraged to perform rites of purification and abstain from meat. They retire to a quiet and secluded place to rest. They minimize desire, do not listen to music, and refrain from sexual activity. Having rested mind and body, they will be ready for the tasks of the next year.

In this month, only the tall grass is left standing. The worms are hidden underground, and the deer are shedding their antlers. Only trees in the vicinity of springs can be felled for firewood and the making of farm equipment. Idle government administrators are dismissed, and surplus equipment is stowed away. Gates and locks in government buildings are inspected, and prison facilities are repaired.

If the rites of summer are performed in the eleventh month, there will be drought. Heavy fog will cover the land, and there will be constant thunder and lightning. If the rites of autumn are performed, there will be excessive rain. Melons and legumes will not ripen, and there will be war and destruction. If the rites of spring are performed, locusts will destroy the crops. The water in the springs will become stale, and there will be epidemics.

The twelfth month is at the end of winter. During this month, life begins to stir. The ravens begin to leave the warmer lands, and many birds prepare to build their nests. The cries of apes, monkeys, and other creatures of the forest are heard, and ducks and hens are ready to lay eggs.

In this month, the farmers are encouraged to breed plow animals and repair plows. The fishing season begins. The amount of grain in storage is recorded, and based on the deficit or surplus, the next season's farming activity is planned. Musicians schedule rehearsals and give public performances. Forests are cleared of fallen branches and dead trees to prepare for spring growth.

By the end of winter, the sun has completed its yearly cycle and the constellations have appeared in the sky in one full cycle. The year has come to an end, and a new one will begin. To allow the citizens to prepare for the coming of the new year, no new government projects are started.

As the year draws to an end, the ruler and the ministers review the laws, the rites, and the rituals. They discuss the past year's achievements and plan the next year's projects. The income of the people is recorded, and every household is asked to contribute a fraction of its income to the offerings at the mountain and valley shrines.

If the rites of autumn are performed in the twelfth month, frost will fall early, snails will multiply, and crops will be ruined. People will abandon the countryside to seek shelter in the towns, and crime and violence will increase. If the rites of spring are performed, there will be birth defects, infant deaths, and illness. If the rites of summer are performed, snow will fall at inappropriate times. The ice on the rivers and lakes will melt early, and there will be floods.

# 4

Sky, Earth, and Humanity

## HUMAN ACTIONS ELICIT RESPONSES FROM THE TAO

It was said that when the musician Guang played the piece "White Clouds" on the zither, cranes alighted on his dwelling, a gentle wind blew, and soft rain fell. When the ruler of Chin was ill, drought ravaged his country and laid waste to thousands of miles of land. In the country of Qi, when a widow who was framed for murder cried for justice, lightning struck the ruler's palace and injured him, hurricanes destroyed the coastal towns, and heavy rains flooded the countryside.

The musician and the widow of Qi were not prominent citizens. Neither were they rich or famous. Yet their actions elicited a response from the celestial realm because they were sincere. The guardians of the celestial realm are aware of everything that happens in the mortal realm. Whether we are in the middle of a dark forest, in the depths of a cave, or inside a locked chamber, we cannot hide our unethical actions and escape retribution. The Tao is always watching.

When King Wen of Zhou (1152–1056 B.C.E.) was fighting the tyrant Cou, his army was stopped by the raging waters of the Meng River. White caps raced on the waters, and the sky was dark with storm clouds. No one, not even his shaman advisers, could see the other shore. King Wen raised his great ax in one hand and waved his banner, crying, "I have taken the responsibility to save the nation from tyranny! Who dares to stop me from achieving my goal?" Suddenly, the wind stopped, the waters calmed, and the army of Zhou was able to cross the river.

The prince of Chu was defeating the despotic ruler of the Han Dynasty in battle when the sun was about to set. Knowing that darkness would help his enemy escape, the prince raised his spear and appealed to celestial lords to give him enough time to capture the hated tyrant. The sun reversed its path and climbed back above the horizon.

## CONNECTING TO THE TAO AND THE CELESTIAL WAY

To value life, to retain the true spirit, to care for the body, and to persevere under the most trying circumstances—these actions are sufficient to elicit empathy from the Tao. If the spirit is in harmony with the Tao, the Tao will respond in support. If the Tao empathizes with warriors who are not afraid of death, how much more will it empathize with people who see the sky and the earth as home, who regard all things as related, and who befriend the forces of yin and yang?

Those whose hearts and minds are in union with the Tao are filled with the vapor of supreme harmony. Outwardly they take on human form, but inwardly they embrace the Tao. Observant and aware of everything, they can understand that which cannot be known. Because they are at one with the Tao, the Tao will stand behind them in everything they do.

Once a musician named Yong was able to use his music to move a prince named Meng to tears. The prince would wipe his eyes and sigh even before he knew what was in his mind. This is because Yong's song was inseparable from his heart, and when he played his music, his feelings reached the prince's heart before any words were spoken.

To be able to reach into another person's heart is not a skill that can be learned. It is attained only when the barrier between the self and the external world is dissolved. If you imitate outward behavior without the true feelings, people will recognize your deception immediately and know you are insincere.

The great archer Bo could hit a bird perched on a building a thousand feet high, and the legendary fisherman Chan could catch a fish from the deepest lake. Having cleared their minds, honed their skills, and focused their wills, they were no longer separated from their targets.

As far as they were concerned, the bird was shot and the fish was caught before the arrow left the bow or the line was dropped into the water.

## ALL THINGS ARE CONNECTED

There is a mysterious force behind the interaction of things that even the most intelligent cannot understand. For example, when the east wind blows, wine becomes stale. When silkworms weave their cocoons, the strings on a zither become brittle and break. When whales die on the beach, shooting stars and natural disasters appear. We don't know why coincidences like these occur. Perhaps everything is interrelated, so that when something happens, it elicits a response from others.

Sagely rulers embrace the natural ways and teach not by speaking but by setting examples. They care for the people and are only interested in leading them in the ways of goodness. Under their leadership, the sun and the moon follow their courses, rain and snow are timely, and disasters are uncommon. However, if the ruler is corrupt and the ministers are rebellious, omens appear in the sky. The five vapors of the sun spread to block out the clear sky. The sun scorches the land, and the rain causes floods. Animals behave strangely, people lose their connection to the natural ways, and there is a need for strict laws and enforcement of order.

Clouds born from mountain vapor appear like swaying grass, clouds born from stream vapor appear like fish scales, clouds born from the hot vapor of the sun appear like smoke, and clouds born from ocean vapor appear like breakers. Each type of cloud has characteristics related to where it originated. This is because everything in the universe is connected.

## YIN AND YANG FOLLOW THE NATURAL WAY

Pure yin is like the coolness of a crisp wind; pure yang is like the heat of the summer sun. When pure yin and pure yang interact, ten thousand things are created. If there was only yang and no yin, or vice versa, there would be no creation. Such is the natural way.

Thus, if you want foreign nations to respect your country, you must follow the natural way and not be intrusive. If you want your subjects to be loyal, you must follow the natural way and instill harmony among them. Let the natural way direct your actions. Be unassuming and accomplish your goals quietly. In this way, there will be peace and stability in the nation. The fields will be cultivated, troops will not have to be sent abroad to fight foreign wars, and the people will be contented. These are the subtle ways of ruling. Faster than the swiftest runner, the interactions of yin and yang play out their course. Sinking and floating, brightening and dimming—their cycles of change all follow the natural way.

It is difficult to heat resin in winter and make ice in summer. In the same manner, you cannot use an herb whose function is to strengthen bones to cure an upset stomach. All these things are difficult, if not impossible, because they run counter to the natural way of things.

## UNDERSTANDING THE NATURAL ORDER

Know the natural order of things, and you will not meet with disaster. The Tao is impartial and has no vested interests. Those who follow it will have more than enough; those who do not follow it will always be lacking. Those who follow the natural way will come to prosperity; those who do not follow it will meet with misfortune. It is hard to measure gain and loss. Depending on the point of view, what is considered by one person as gain may be considered by another as loss. Therefore, we should not argue over gain and loss or let it direct our lives. In the Tao, there is no gain and loss, no success or failure; there are only circumstances and events that we evaluate and measure from our point of view.

We can use fire to melt metal and burn wood. However, we cannot use a magnet to attract clay. Each thing has its function. Use an object according to its natural function, and you will succeed. Use it to do something that it was not made to do, and you will not accomplish anything.

Rubbing flint together can make fire, a magnet can attract iron, and sunflowers turn toward light—these things happen naturally. Even the most intelligent people do not know why.

You cannot understand the nature of things using the senses and the intellect. You cannot distinguish truth from falsehood by looking at things from your personal perspective. Only those who are in tune with the natural order of things can intuitively know what will happen. When there are landslides, rivers will be blocked. When there are master sword makers, there will be superior weapons. When ministers are corrupt, tyrants will appear. When a ruler is assisted by wise advisers, great deeds will be accomplished. This is the natural way of things. Given the circumstances, we cannot force the outcomes to be otherwise.

## PART TWO

# The Taoist in Domestic Life

## The Art of Healthy Living: Embracing Simplicity

Teachings from *Principles of Nourishing Life and Cultivating Longevity, Peng Zu's Method of Prolonging Life*, and *Embracing Simplicity*

# 5

# Understanding the Energy of Life

Laozi said the following: The valley spirit that does not die is the Mysterious Female. The gate of the Mysterious Female is the root of the sky and the earth.

Heshang Gong (202–157 B.C.E.), known as the Sage of the River, added the following: *Valley* means protection. If we are able to protect the spirit, we will live long and never die. The spirit guards the five viscera. Within the liver is the luminous spirit; within the lungs is the soul; within the kidneys is the generative essence; within the heart is the essence of intelligence; within the spleen is the spirit of feelings and intention. If any of these organs is injured, the guardian of that viscus will leave. As a result, life energy will be harmed, and health will deteriorate.

The key to longevity lies in the Mysterious Female. What is the Mysterious Female? *Mysterious* refers to the sky. In the senses, it is the nostrils. *Female* refers to the earth. In the senses, it is the mouth. The vapor of the sky enters through the nostrils and is stored in the heart. This vapor is fresh and subtle. When it enters and resides in the heart, it makes us intelligent and wise. However, when coupled with discursive thought, it gives rise to excitement, anger, desire, fear, and anxiety. The ruler of these feelings is male in nature. Entering through the nostrils, the vapor of the sky interacts with the vapor stored in the heart. Exiting through the nostrils, the vapor of the heart returns to the sky.

The earth provides us with food and is the source of the five flavors: sweet, sour, bitter, spicy, and salty. The vapor of the earth enters through the mouth and resides in the liver. The five flavors interact with the muscles, the bones, and the blood, and when coupled with feelings give rise to happiness, anger, sorrow, delight, love, and hate. The ruler of these six feelings is female in nature. Entering through the mouth, the vapor of the earth interacts with the vapor stored in the liver. Exiting through the mouth, the vapor of the liver returns to the earth.

The cycles of inhalation and exhalation are intimately tied to the interactive exchange between the vapors of the sky and the earth and the vapors of the body. The nostrils and the mouth are the orifices where the primordial vapors of the sky and the earth enter the human body. Primordial vapor enters the body as the subtle breath, which is soft and elusive. To absorb the vapors of the sky and the earth, inhalation and exhalation must be natural and not forced. Only in this way can the vapors of the sky and the earth enter the body to nourish the internal organs.

Distance yourself from desire, and you will live a long and healthy life. Let desire run your life, and the spirit will lose its brightness. When the spirit loses its luminosity, the production of the generative essence will be compromised. When the generative essence is low, the body will weaken. With the continued weakening of the spirit and the body, there will be no alternative but early death.

There are nine orifices in the body: two eyes, two nostrils, two ears, the mouth, the anus, and the sexual orifice. If you want to live a long and healthy life, you must make sure that the life energy does not leak out from these openings. Constant stimulation of the senses—sight, sound, smell, taste, and touch—can dissipate the life energy stored in the internal organs. Unregulated sexual activity can lead to generative energy exiting through the sexual orifice, and unhealthy eating and drinking habits can force life energy out through the anus.

Some people die early because their lives are too rich and luxurious. They desire too much and try too hard to get what they want. Not knowing contentment, they distance themselves from the simple and natural ways. Taxing mind and body, they expend more energy than they can gather in. Consequently, they use up energy that should be conserved for maintaining health in their later years.

It is said that those who are adept at cultivating and nourishing their life energy will not meet with harm. Animals won't attack them in the wild, robbers won't menace them, and weapons will not kill them. This is not because they are protected by mysterious and magical forces but because they don't get themselves into harmful situations in the first place. In harmony with the natural world, they automatically avoid the paths of hungry predators. Not displaying their wealth, they do not attract robbers. And knowing the nature of danger, they never find themselves in adverse situations.

The human body is like a country, divided into regions. The body has three regions. The first region is the head, and its seat of government, or palace, is the upper elixir field (energy center). The second region is the area around the heart, and its seat of the government is the middle elixir field. The third region is the abdomen, and its seat of government is located in the lower elixir field. The ruler spends time with these three seats of government, like an emperor visiting the provinces of the country to learn about the needs of the people.

The limbs constitute the border regions of the country, and the joints, tendons, muscles, and ligaments are the local officials. The circulatory pathways are the roads and rivers that connect the areas of the country, transporting supplies according to the needs of each region.

If you want to nourish the energy of life, you must understand the principles of ruling. Like an enlightened ruler, the spirit must guide the ministers (the blood, the internal organs, and the skeletal system) and love the people (the life energy). If the ruler fails to oversee the ministers, there will be corruption. If the ruler does not love the people, public works will be neglected, the borders will be unprotected, and there will be social disorder, natural disasters, and invasion. Similarly, if the spirit does not guide the flow of blood, the internal organs will be robbed of nutrients, the circulatory pathways will be blocked, the musculoskeletal system will weaken, and the body will suffer from illness. If the body is unable to ward off illness and disease, then, like a country with no border protection, it will be invaded. If the invaders cannot be driven out, the people will die, the government will fall, and the nation will cease to exist.

Thus, those who value the energy of life need to understand the importance of strengthening it. Nourish the energy of life while you are still healthy. Take preventative measures. Do not wait until the symptoms of illness, disease, and weakness appear. In a strong nation, the citizens are content, the economy is prosperous, the granaries are full, the roads are safe, the garrisons are staffed, the ministers are virtuous, and the ruler is enlightened. Similarly, in a healthy body, the life energy is strong and plentiful, the body is tireless, the internal organs are healthy, the circulatory pathways are open, the limbs are strong and agile, the blood is healthy, and the spirit is bright and clear.

That which guides the natural course of celestial movements is the law of yin and yang. That which regulates the movement of the earth and the cycles of the seasons is the principle of softness and hardness. That which fosters the peace and harmony of human society is virtue. Humans are born from the copulation of the energies of yin and yang. Within the human body is the seed of the Tao, and this seed is the energy of life. Living between the sky and the earth and moving with the four seasons, humans have a short life span compared to that of the mountains and the seas. But rather than feel despair about our short time in the mortal realm, we should value the human body that we are born with.

It is said that of all sentient beings, humans have the strongest potential to realize the Tao. We should therefore develop this potential by valuing the life energy. To value life energy means to conserve, cultivate, and nourish it by living a simple and contented life as well as by practicing the arts of longevity. Practicing the arts of longevity requires discipline, trust, and respect for the teachings. Most important, it requires dissolving negative thoughts and emotions such as ambition, aggression, anger, arrogance, possessiveness, and jealousy. All the teachings of Taoism come down to this.

The primordial energy of the Tao within accumulates naturally in the head when thoughts are extinguished. The area where the primordial energy congregates is called the Mudball cavity, and it is located in the forehead slightly above the area between the two eyes. This cavity rules over the internal organs, the circulatory pathways, and the musculoskeletal system, and it has the power to allocate resources in the body to defend it from illness and disease. When the Mudball cavity abides in stillness, it can stabilize the life energy and stimulate the pro-

duction of the generative essence. Therefore, those who practice the
of longevity should know the importance of cultivating and abiding in
stillness.

Spirit is the root of life, and the body is the vessel. If the spirit is
taxed, it will wither. If the body is stressed, it will weaken and die. If you
tax the spirit with excessive thinking and tire the body with excessive
labor, how can you live long and be healthy? The sages were able to live
long and contented lives because they knew that both spirit and body
need to be preserved and nourished. They also understood that spirit
and body cannot be separated. The separation of body from spirit is
death. Once we die, any return to life in the same body is impossible.
This is why those who value life nourish both body and spirit, in order
to live out their life span fully.

The principles of cultivating the energy of life are sometimes difficult to grasp. However, if you have an inkling that the path to life is the
opposite of the path of indulgence, excessiveness, and scheming, then
you're on the right track. With time, you'll come to understand that
simplicity and moderation are the key to attaining longevity, health,
and happiness.

# 6

# Healthy Attitude, Healthy Lifestyle

Liezi advised the following: When you're young, don't spend a lot of energy doing what everybody thinks is appropriate. When you've reached maturity, don't be too competitive. When you're past middle age, you should begin to find contentment. When you're old, you should minimize desires. Exercise the body gently to prevent it from stiffening, and entertain your mind leisurely to prevent it from deteriorating. In this way, you will enjoy a healthy and long life. Birth, growth, aging, and death are related to the rise and fall of vapor in our bodies, which in turn is related to the primordial breath of life that pervades nature. If we are in tune with the breath of the sky and the earth, we will be able to resonate with the breath of life. The best way to attain health and longevity is to be calm and centered in the midst of turmoil, be free from desire and attachment, and maintain a harmonious relationship with the vapor and breath of the universe.

People get ill and die before their time because they have distanced themselves from the Tao, not because the Tao has distanced itself from them. The primordial life energy never deserts us; it is we who choose to abandon the essence of life. Therefore, the adepts of the arts of health and longevity are careful not to stray from the Tao.

Zhuangzi said the following: The primordial energy of life has no limits. However, there is a limit to knowledge and conceptual thinking. If we use that which has limits to understand that which has no limits, we will end up tiring body and mind. When body and mind are taxed, life energy will weaken, and the span of life will diminish.

People often think that they need to scheme and compete to get what they want. This is because the wayward mind has taken over their lives. The wayward mind is devoted to only one thing: fulfilling its desires. If we are free from the clutches of the wayward mind, we will return to the natural disposition of simplicity. The spirit knows contentment and understands the limits of conceptual thinking. In contrast, the wayward mind is arrogant and thinks that it is powerful and limitless. The wayward mind is so delusional that it believes that ants can move rocks. Consequently, it will not hesitate to expend energy and sacrifice the body to get what it wants. To be dominated by the wayward mind is the surest way to deplete energy and shorten the life span.

Those who understand that life is precious will not engage in activity that harms life. Those who understand destiny will not force themselves to do what they cannot do. Let life run its natural course. Do not interfere with it, and we will each live out our natural life span. On the contrary, if we try to force body and mind to do what they are not endowed to do, we will forfeit what we have been given at birth, expending the energy that has been allotted to us for life in half that time.

The natural way of the Tao is to give birth to and nourish all things. When growth reaches its maximum, it will give way to decline; when decline reaches its limit, growth will begin again, and life will be renewed. Humans know only growth and decline, not renewal. They think that by producing offspring, they are assured of immortality by having descendants. Consequently, after they have borne or sired children, they continue to waste their generative energy. They don't know that when their generative energy is depleted, they will die.

Worse, they don't know that spirit energy is the source of generative energy. Thoughts expend the energy of the spirit, and when the spirit is exhausted it will no longer produce generative energy. When generative energy is low, the body will weaken and be vulnerable to illness. Eventually, when the last drop of generative energy is gone, the body will not be able to sustain itself, and the person will die.

Conservation of generative energy is therefore the first step to enhancing health and prolonging life. In addition, if you cultivate and replenish generative energy by nourishing the spirit, you will be able to age with the sun, the moon, and the stars and be renewed with the seasons. Suspending conceptual thought and minimizing desire can focus and strengthen the spirit. When the spirit is strengthened, generative energy will naturally be plentiful. When generative energy is plentiful, the body will naturally be protected from disease and illness.

Rest in stillness, and let the body sink into the subtle vapor of life. Leave your thoughts in places you will not visit, and let yourself return to the natural way. Live in simplicity and abide in stillness, and you will be able to penetrate the mysteries of creation and dissolution, existence and nonexistence. Merging with the sky and the earth, you will be able to live a long time.

We are endowed with the primordial vapor of the Tao at birth. Why is it that some people live long whereas others die early? Why are some strong and others weak? Why are some people more intelligent than others? Is our destiny determined by the will of heaven, or are we responsible for our own disposition and fortune?

Intelligence is endowed by heaven. However, longevity and health are not predetermined. Although birth, growth, and death are part of natural existence, how we live our lives—healthy or unhealthy, long or short—is entirely in our hands.

A fetus that did not receive sufficient nourishment in the mother's womb may be born weak and sickly. However, if care and nourishment are given during infancy and childhood, if generative energy is conserved after puberty, if spirit is cultivated during adulthood, and if physical strength and mental clarity are established through meditation and *qigong* exercises, that baby can live a long and healthy life. This is called using postcreation methods to repair precreation inadequacies.

A fetus that has received sufficient nourishment in the mother's womb is likely to be born healthy. However, if insufficient nourishment is given during infancy and childhood, if generative energy is wasted after puberty, if the energy of the spirit is expended in adulthood by excessive thinking and scheming, and if physical strength and mental clarity are not cultivated, that baby will not live a healthy and long life. This is called ruining precreation endowment with postcreation actions.

Thus, if a person lives a short and unhealthy life, it is not because destiny has decreed it but because he or she has lived a lifestyle of eating unhealthy foods, indulging in too much sex and alcohol, and scheming too much after fame and fortune. Similarly, if a person lives a healthy and long life, it is not because it has been decreed by destiny but because he or she has lived a life of simplicity and contentment. Conserving the generative essence by regulating sexual activity, nourishing the breath of life by practicing *qigong*, and cultivating the spirit through stillness, the person is able to live a long and healthy life in happiness and contentment.

Those who belittle the powers of nature and its seasonal transformations will meet with calamities. Those who understand and follow the ways of the natural world will be able to harvest its gifts. In spring and summer, you should live in the highlands and mountains to take in the cool air. Spend time outdoors, especially in the morning and the evening. Rise early and finish working before noon. Stay up late and enjoy the night breeze. Eat and sleep less. Too much food and sleep on warm days can dim your consciousness and make you lethargic. The best times to meditate are late at night and early in the morning.

In autumn and winter, you should live in lower altitudes. Don't expose yourself to chilly air and cold winds. Spend more time indoors, especially in the morning and the evening. Rise late and finish working before daylight fades. Go to bed early and eat and sleep more. Not eating enough on cold days can weaken the body and muddle your thoughts. Winter is the natural time of rest. Thus, it is the best season for retreating into yourself and spending your days meditating.

People in ancient times tapped their teeth together* and swallowed saliva to nourish their internal organs. They regulated their breath, circulated their energy, and ingested the vapors of the sky and the earth to vitalize their muscles, joints, and tendons. Engage in these practices regularly, and your limbs will be agile and strong and your internal organs will be whole and healthy. When the five viscera and the six bowels (bladder, gall bladder, stomach, large intestine, small intestine, and the triple heater meridian) function harmoniously, you will be protected from disease and illness and live a long and healthy life.

Scheming, desiring, hating, worrying, acting recklessly, talking loudly, being rude and boisterous, being uncontrollably excited and

---

* This is a *qigong* practice that vibrates the qi in the head.

elated, and living in fear and doubt can destroy life energy. Minimizing these actions is the key to nourishing life.

Too much thinking and scheming damages the spirit. Too much desire can make us anxious and indecisive. Excessive talking and boisterous behavior harm intelligence and reduce mental clarity. Too much physical activity weakens the bones and tendons. Too much talk disrupts the natural rhythm of the breath. An angry disposition harms the heart. Being easily excited or depressed damages the liver and lungs, and being hateful blocks circulation in the meridians.

In general, a life with moderate physical and mental activity tends to be healthy. People who don't worry too much or want too much are more likely to live long lives. On the contrary, people who are concerned about getting ahead, becoming famous, and getting rich usually end up living short and unhappy lives. People who have the means to indulge in luxuries often live less healthy lives than those who don't, and hermits live longer than those who actively seek fame. This is because the more complicated the lifestyle, the more energy is expended. We expend energy when we are angry, competitive, anxious, worried, and devious. We expend energy when we hate, fear, desire, and argue. If energy is spent feeding these attitudes, there won't be much left to nourish the internal organs, the bones, and the tendons. If you are able to devote your time to cultivating and nourishing more energy, you can live a much healthier and longer life.

Health begins with clearing the senses. The eyes should not stare at things that attract you. The ears should not be exposed to loud and dissonant noises. Do not subject the nose to smells that are pungent or that reek of blood. Do not gorge on food that is overly spicy. Do not direct your mental activity to scheming and thinking negative thoughts. Staring at things that attract you increases desire. Loud and distractive noises disturb inner peace. Decaying smells pollute the lungs and disrupt the natural circulation of breath. Foods that burn the mouth can traumatize the stomach and intestines. Negative thoughts and attitudes muddy the clarity of thoughts and disrupt inner balance and harmony.

In the morning, do not sigh and complain about your problems. Think positively about yourself and others the moment you rise. At night, don't raise your voice or argue; this will churn up negative energy and prevent you from having a restful night.

Although it is not practical for everyone to be a hermit, it is possible to live a peaceful and simple life earning a livelihood that can support you and your family. The key to preserving life energy lies in minimizing desire, knowing the limits of the body, maintaining clarity, and having a peaceful disposition. You can make a living without having to scheme and think negative thoughts. Allow things to happen rather than trying to force things to go your way. If you live a life of moderation and contentment, you won't feel overexcited when things work to your benefit or be terribly disappointed when things don't work out.

Those who have a peaceful disposition typically live longer than those who are hot-tempered. This is because anger, aggression, and impatience can drain energy. However, if fiery-tempered people are willing to cultivate a peaceful countenance, they will be able to conserve their life energy as effectively as those who are peaceful and patient. If those who already have a peaceful disposition are able to cultivate their life energy further by stilling their thoughts and strengthening the body, they will age with the sun, the moon, and the stars.

The Yellow Emperor (2698–2598 B.C.E.) asked his adviser Qi Ba the following: I've heard that in ancient times people lived long and healthy lives. Even at a hundred, their faces glowed, their complexion was smooth, their limbs were agile, and they were rarely ill. Nowadays people are weak and unhealthy before they're fifty. Their limbs are no longer agile, their spines are misaligned, their internal organs do not function properly, and the circulation of their internal energy is sluggish. What made the ancient peoples happier and healthier than we are?

Qi Ba replied as follows: In ancient days, people understood the principles of yin and yang. They lived according to the cycle of the seasons and the waxing and waning of the sun and the moon. They rose with the sun and rested at sunset. They ate healthy foods and practiced *qigong* to build resistance to seasonal illness. They regulated sexual activity, did not labor excessively, and never entertained negative thoughts. Thus, life energy was conserved, and the spirit was calm and peaceful. Today, people do not understand the workings of yin and yang. They scheme tirelessly to get things they want but do not need. They eat foods that harm rather than nourish their bodies. They indulge in excessive sexual activity, they drink liquor like water, they are angered easily, and worse, they are aggressive and impatient. Trying to satisfy material needs in the short term, they dissipate life energy by pushing body and spirit beyond their limits. They don't know that true happiness and contentment do not lie in material things and sexual pleasure. Nature lasts forever because it knows how to renew itself. Even animals know how to preserve their energy by hibernating in winter and procreating only at specific times of the year. Humans, however, have lost their connection with the cyclical rhythms of life in the natural world and are living against the principles of the waxing and waning of yin and yang. How can you expect people nowadays to live long and stay healthy?

Laozi once said that it is common for people to live to be a hundred if they abstain from excesses. If you are able to still your thoughts, relax the body, and practice *qigong*, you too can live a long and healthy life. The life span is like an oil lamp. The lamp comes with a full reservoir of oil when it is new. A lamp that burns with a bright flame will use more oil and extinguish sooner than one that burns with a soft flame. Similarly, if we use too much energy in the early part of our lives, our lives will be short. A lamp that burns constantly will extinguish sooner than one that burns only periodically.

If we know how to rest and conserve energy, our lives will be longer and healthier. If the lamp is given a continuous supply of oil, it can burn for an indefinitely long time. Understanding this, the sages knew the importance of cultivating and conserving their life force, and in doing so, they were able to remain healthy and live beyond the normal life span.

Our life energy will be strong and plentiful if we maintain a low voice while others shout, if we are relaxed while others fret, if we are calm while others are angry, if we are generous while others are greedy, if we are not affected by daily petty concerns, if we don't engage in work that demands excessive physical or mental effort, and if we are able to understand and follow the natural way of things rather than force things to fit our plans.

People nowadays get ill easily and die early because they don't know how to conserve energy. They spend their lives competing with others to win fame, fortune, and recognition. Aggression, anger, greed, jealousy, pride, competitiveness, and desire are poisonous. They can weaken the joints, muscles, tendons, and bones; damage the internal organs and block the circulation of energy; and muddy the clarity of thoughts. When the body is tired and broken, when the organs are dysfunctional, when circulation is blocked, and when mental activity is feeble and thoughts are unclear, all kinds of illnesses will arise. The bright and clear vapor of life will wane, and the dark vapor of death and decay will take over. When we are completely overrun by the dark vapor, we will die.

The key to prolonging life lies in not worrying about what to wear and what to eat and drink. Stay away from excessive socializing, regulate sexual activity, do not be attached to gain and loss, and do not be concerned with reputation and social recognition. If you are able to do these things, your spirit will be centered and calm. If the spirit is calm, you will be relaxed. If you are relaxed, energy will flow freely in your body. When energy flows without obstruction, the internal organs will be nourished and the skeletal system will be strengthened. In addition, if you are able to nourish your body by doing *qigong* and still the mind by practicing meditation, your life span will be long beyond imagination.

Do not be distracted by desire, emotions, and conceptions. Think but don't scheme. Appreciate things around you but do not crave them. Use your speech to communicate and not to slander. Exercise your body but do not tire it. Live in simplicity and contentment, and you'll be healthier and happier than those who do not.

Those who crave power and control will tire both body and spirit, even if they are ethical in their dealings. If you start out wealthy but lose your fortune later in life, you're bound to be frustrated and disappointed. Some will even lose their will to live. If you start out poor but end up accumulating wealth, you're likely to be extravagant. Like a starving person gorging food, you'll wallow in newfound luxuries. However, if you are able to treat gain and loss with stride, you won't feel despondent if you lose your fortune or ecstatic when you find it. In this way, the spirit will remain calm. When the spirit is calm, the body will be relaxed, and when the body is relaxed, life energy will be preserved.

Exercising in winter can warm the blood and enhance the circulation of energy. Resting in summer can reduce the threat of heatstroke. This is what is meant by harmonizing the workings of yin and yang in the body with the seasons.

The key to preserving life lies in not walking too much, not sitting too much, not sleeping too much, not thinking too much, and not stimulating the senses too much. Also, don't overeat, don't get intoxicated, and don't get too attached to gain and loss. Follow the principle of moderation, and you will live a long and healthy life.

The destiny of our lives is in our hands, not in others', nor is it in a deity's. Those who do not understand this are doomed to suffer ill health and die before their time. Many people don't value their life energy, and therefore they waste it by indulging in pleasure and material things. Others value their life energy but keep putting off conserving it. And some don't even know that life energy is intimately linked to life span. If you don't know how to conserve life energy, you'll end up spending most of it before you reach middle age.

If you use all the nutrients in the soil for your grove in one season, the trees will have no nourishment in future years and will wither and die. If you neglect to repair small leaks in a dam, the structure will burst without warning, and you will drown. Managing an orchard and repairing a dam are things you can do; they are not determined by the stars you were born under or the will of any deities. Similarly, the choice of conserving or wasting your life energy is yours to make. If you value your life, you should calm your spirit, dissolve your desires, and relax your body. It's not uncommon for people to live a long time without illness if they know how to conserve life energy.

The principles of conserving the energy of life can be summed up as follows: Preserve generative energy by regulating sexual activity; nourish the spirit by regulating mental activity; cultivate vital energy by minimizing speech; care for the body by not subjecting it to extreme activities, by practicing the techniques of enhancing life (such as *qigong* and meditation), and by not eating or sleeping too much. Do not be attached to gain and loss and social recognition, do not harbor negative thoughts, and do not engage in activities that hurt others.

It is not healthy to be inactive. If you don't move frequently, the body will weaken. If you're bored, your intelligence will be dulled. If the spirit wanders, it will become wayward. However, it is also unhealthy to push physical and mental activities to the extreme. If you try to lift weights beyond what your body can handle, run or swim beyond what your body can endure, or neglect to rest after heavy physical labor, you will damage your joints, muscles, tendons, and bones. If you try to solve problems beyond your mental capacity, force yourself to learn that which is beyond your intellect, or neglect to rest after long hours of mental activity, you will injure your spirit and generative essence.

Nourish and relax the body with *qigong* exercises. Calm the spirit with meditation. Yang starts to rise at eleven o'clock at night, and yin begins to rise at eleven in the morning. At these times, spirit and body should be at rest to allow a smooth transition between the waning of one vapor and the waxing of the other. In between these critical times, engage in a balance of physical and mental activity. Lethargic inactivity is like a pool of stagnant water filled with decaying vegetation. However, water that is constantly stormy also cannot support life. A healthy lifestyle always balances movement and stillness. That's why it is good to take walks after meals. A mild and relaxing activity helps the digestion of food. If activity and inactivity are not balanced, food will not be digested properly. As a result, the circulation of energy in the meridians will be sluggish, and spirit and body will become dull and lazy. Knowing the principle of balance is important in maintaining health and longevity.

Rest before you feel tired. By the time you feel fatigue, the reserve energy in the body will have been used. Consequently, you'd have to rest longer to replenish what was spent from storage. Eat before you feel famished. Otherwise the food will appear excessively attractive and you will overeat. Stop eating before you feel full. By the time you feel satiated, you will have eaten more than what your digestive system can handle. Don't overstimulate your sense of taste by eating foods that have too many flavors. Generally, it is better to eat too little than to overeat.

Go to bed before you feel sleepy. Allow the body to relax and let your thoughts slow down before you fall asleep. Do not be physically and mentally active just before bedtime. Mental activity stirs up conceptual thinking, and physical activity heats up the blood, thus preventing you from resting effectively. Travel in a vehicle only if the distance is too great to walk. Think when you really need to think. Talk only when you need to communicate. Balance action with nonaction, movement with stillness, and you'll find that living a long, healthy, and contented life is not so hard after all.

The methods of cultivating health and longevity are the same as those that protect body and spirit. Keep warm in the winter and cool in the summer. Do not engage in activities or eat foods that are inappropriate for the seasons. In all things, achieve a sense of balance and moderation. This is the great secret to living a long and healthy life.

If you always wear a lot of clothing and cover yourself with thick blankets when you sleep, your body will never have the chance to temper itself. Consequently, it will become ill with the slightest chill. If you always eat rich food, if you never miss a meal, and if you reach for snacks even when you are not hungry, you are bound to have digestion and weight problems. If you cannot bear to not have sex for even a few days, your generative energy will be depleted, and your skin will take on a dry, dark pallor. This is because the generative essence that is the source of youthfulness will have no time to regenerate and moisten your skin and brighten your complexion.

Listen to loud music all day, and your hearing will suffer. Tax your eyesight, and your acuity will decrease. Frequent participation in sports that arouse excitement can dull your thinking. Having negative attitudes and scheming to take advantage of others can drain your life energy. Often we don't know we are injured until it's too late. This is because we wait for the body to give us signals of pain and discomfort before we acknowledge that there is a problem. The causes of injuries and illness are usually planted way before the symptoms emerge, and these causes usually stem from an unhealthy lifestyle.

The sages lived long and healthy lives because they understood contentment and stayed away from activities that harm body and spirit. They knew that activity and nonactivity are like fire and water. You must not have too much of either. Fire can warm us, but if it is out of control, it will burn us. No one can live without water, but if we are immersed in water permanently, we will drown.

There are three great causes of illness: excessive sexual activity, grasping after wealth and material things, and gossip and slander. Excessive sexual desire is blind to love and caring because the partner is seen only as an object of satisfying desire. When one's regular partner is not available or is uninterested, sexual craving will lead to affairs with other people's loved ones without consideration of whether it will cause suffering. Thoughts and dreams of sexual pleasure can drain generative energy as much as the activity itself. Therefore, the initial loss of life energy stems from the inability to distinguish sexual possessiveness from caring love.

Greed does not know satiation. Needs can be satisfied, but wants can never be fulfilled. With greed, the more you attain, the more you will crave, and the more you crave, the more you will scheme to satisfy those cravings. The loss of life energy, therefore, is intimately related to the inability to distinguish wants from needs.

Slander is rooted in jealousy, envy, anger, and aggression. Fabrication of events and people's actions lie at the heart of slander. When a lie is told, more lies will have to be told to cover the previous lie. With time, you will find yourself doing nothing but spinning false stories to cover up reality. This kind of mental fabrication damages the brightness of the spirit. When energy that should be allotted to nourishing life energy is used to create cover-up stories, how can we expect slanderers to be healthy?

The key to good health and long life lies in valuing life. Harm others, and you'll eventually harm yourself. Take advantage of others, and you'll be the loser in the long run. Having a peaceful disposition and doing good deeds are the foundations of health and longevity. If this foundation is absent, the techniques of improving health—such as massage, breath regulation, and calisthenics—will yield few or no results.

Excessive elation and excitement can lead to the spirit becoming wayward. Excessive sadness can block the circulation of blood. Mental exertion can lead to chronic fatigue and frequent headaches. Overuse of the eyes can lead to loss of acuity. Oversleeping can lead to depression and lethargy. Overeating can lead to dysfunction of all the internal organs, not just the stomach and intestines. Today, people want to eat only what delights them. They can't tell the difference between foods that harm and those that nourish. Consequently, they develop illnesses that are associated with eating the wrong foods. Those who understand the principles of conserving life energy will eat foods that are nourishing and avoid those that block the flow of energy. Moreover, understanding that energy can be dissipated through the mouth, they speak only when necessary and refrain from useless chatting. In this way, their life energy will always be plentiful.

After perspiring, do not sit or lie down for a long time, because this can lead to deterioration of the joints and the back muscles. Rest for a bit and then engage in a gentle relaxing activity to keep the body moving. In this way, the circulation of blood will not be sluggish. Also, after exerting yourself in the heat, do not douse yourself with cold water, because this can lead to rheumatism. Do not drink ice water after perspiring profusely; drink lukewarm water. Wait until you've stopped perspiring before you drink cold liquids. You'll be surprise that doing these simple things can be of tremendous help in strengthening your immunity to illness and disease. Do not sing at the top of your voice or talk loudly and animatedly before you go to sleep. Such activities stir up the spirit and do not allow it to relax and rest. Do not work, talk, or eat immediately after you wake up. Otherwise, the life energy will be damaged.

Do not put a heater next to your head while you sleep. Otherwise, your sleep will be too heavy, and it will be difficult to wake up. If you sleep with a breeze constantly blowing at your head, your spirit will be disturbed, and you will not get a good rest. Moreover, chronic headaches can occur if the head is chilled. Do not leave a light on in the bedroom while you sleep. This will confuse the spirit and not allow it to relax.

In winter, you should cover your feet and your shoulders while you are sleeping to keep them warm. The head, however, should never be covered during sleep. In the other seasons, both the head and the feet should be left uncovered in bed so that the body can cool naturally. You should not open your mouth while you sleep, because vital energy will leak out with exhalation.

After waking, do not wash yourself with cold water. Even in hot weather, you should wash with lukewarm water. If you wake up in the middle of the night thirsty, do not drink cold water. Lukewarm water is preferable.

When you sleep, you should bend your legs slightly. The leg closer to the bed should be straighter than the leg on top. In this way, the tendons and muscles will be relaxed during sleep, allowing the blood to circulate. Do not sleep on your stomach, because this puts strain on your internal organs.

If you see or hear someone having nightmares, do not turn on the light. Wake the person gently with soft words. A gentle touch on the shoulders is also recommended.

In winter, all things in nature are at rest. We too should preserve and protect our internal energy by refraining from heavy physical and mental activity. Thus, winter should be a time for meditation and retreat from the world. Spring is the time for planning and initiating projects. However, do not launch into a heavy work schedule then, because your body and your mind need a gentle transition from rest into engaging with the world. Summer is the time for heightened activity. Just when the sun is at its height, your activities should be strong and radiant. Autumn is the time for harvesting the fruits of projects begun in spring and nourished in summer. Do not start new projects. Complete the existing work and prepare for retreat in the winter. Follow this regimen, and your life energy will rise and fall according to the natural waxing and waning of the vapors of the universe. Rested in winter and renewed in spring, you will be able to age with the sun and the moon and regenerate with the cycle of the seasons.

If you want to nourish life, you must value your internal energies. The body is like a nation. Spirit energy is the ruler, blood and fluids are the ministers, and life energy is the citizenry. If a ruler loves the people, the nation will be strong and prosperous. Similarly, if you cultivate vital energy, the body will be nourished. If the people of a nation are destitute, the country will be in ruins. Similarly, if life energy is weak, we will be ill.

Life energy is cultivated by being nonattached to fame, excitement, materialism, luxury, negativity, and jealousy. Minimize thoughts, memories, laughter, speech, elation, anger, excitement, worry, greed, fear, aggression, control, and scheming, and you'll be able to sustain the life energy within.

Do not sit too long, walk too much, or stand too long. Do not overstimulate the five senses. Do not overeat, do not indulge in luxuries, do not deceive, do not be competitive, and do not belittle others. If you can do this, you will be content. If you are content, the body will naturally be filled with vital energy, and you will live a long and healthy life.

There are six things you can do in your daily life that will help you nourish and cultivate life energy. First, distance yourself from fame, fortune, and power. Second, minimize listening to dissonant sounds and do not indulge in sexual excess.* Third, do not be attached to material things. Fourth, do not crave rich foods. Fifth, abandon vanity, deceit, anger, and recklessness. Sixth, dissolve jealousy and refrain from slander and gossip. If you are unable to cultivate internal energy in your daily life, then no matter how hard you study the arts of longevity, how much you ingest herbs, or how diligent you are in practicing *qigong*, you will not be able to attain health and well-being.

Follow the natural ways of simplicity and contentment by minimizing thought, worry, loud laughter, speech, elation, anger, excitement,

---

* These two items are listed together in the text because it is known that sexual energy is dissipated by listening to dissonant sounds.

anxiety, desire, hate, physical activity, and scheming. Too much thinking will weaken the spirit. Too much worrying will tire the heart. Too
much loud laughter will send shocks through the internal organs. Too
much speech will weaken the vital energy. Too much elation will damage the bladder. Too much anger will weaken the tendons and muscles
as well as agitate the blood. Too much excitement will diminish the
ability to focus. Too much anxiety will lead to loss of hair. Too much
desire will weaken the bones. Too much hate will lead to erratic flow of
the blood. Too much physical activity will block the blood vessels. Too
much scheming will lead to confused thinking. All these activities
shorten the life span. Like an ax, they cut deep into your health and
longevity. They are more dangerous than the most ferocious animals.

Do not sit too long. Do not walk too much. Do not tire your eyes.
Do not be exposed constantly to harsh sounds. If you eat only when you
are famished, the spleen will weaken. If you drink only when you are
extremely thirsty, the stomach will weaken. The body needs regular
movement for it to be strong. However, it should not be strained and
overworked. Intake of food should be moderate. In winter, you should
never go without breakfast. In summer, you should not eat too much in
the evening.

If you are able to deal with everything with a peaceful mind, your
life energy will naturally be nourished. If you are dishonest and un-
trustworthy, your spirit will become dim. If you argue with others, your
spirit will become agitated and lose its clarity. Being aggressive and
angry could deduct years from your life span. If others die or are injured
for your pleasure and enjoyment, the life spans of those you have taken
will be subtracted from yours. Do a good deed, and your spirit will soar.
Do a harmful deed, and the monsters that feast on your life energy will
be happy. If you are able to live a life of simplicity and contentment,
your body will be relaxed, and you will enjoy inner peace. This is the
most effective way of protecting yourself from disease and illness.

Embrace softness and distance yourself from power, and your spirit
will be strong. If the spirit is strong, you will live a long and healthy
life. If you are ambitious and arrogant, your vital energy will be roused
and will dissipate. Consequently, your health will deteriorate. The arts
of health and longevity are about strengthening the spirit and stabiliz-
ing the vital energy. Be moderate in all activities. If your behavior is

extreme and if your thoughts, emotions, and desires are exces.
energy will be spent, and your life span will shorten.

Worrying about things that are beyond your control will h
spirit's confidence. Forcing yourself to do things that are beyon
physical ability will injure the body. Laugh too hard, and the internal
organs will suffer. Sit too long, and the muscular system will weaken.
Sleep too much, and the liver will be harmed. Work too much, and the
spleen will weaken. If you are preoccupied with getting more and ac-
complishing more, the spirit will not be able to rest. If the spirit is unable to rest, life energy cannot be replenished. If life energy is not
replenished, it will diminish daily. When your life energy is completely
spent, you will die.

Don't walk too fast, because this will injure your muscles, joints,
and tendons. Constant exposure to loud and dissonant sounds and pro-
longed viewing of images can harm the sense organs. Do not sit too long
or sleep too long. Put on clothing immediately when you feel a chill.
Shed clothing when you feel warm. Eat before you feel famished. Stop
eating before you feel full. Drink before you feel thirsty. Food and drink
should be taken in moderation. If you eat too much, the food will not be
digested properly and will turn toxic in the stomach and the intestines.
If you drink too much, the kidneys and bladder will be damaged.

Don't be too busy or too lazy. A moderate amount of physical and
mental activity will keep the body strong and the thoughts clear. Too
much activity, however, will tire body and spirit and tax the vital energy. Do not engage in physical activity that makes you perspire too
much. Perspiration in the right amount will clear the pores, but excessive perspiration will dissipate generative energy and damage bone
marrow. Do not engage in rigorous physical and mental activity immediately after eating. Do not force yourself to eat when you don't have an
appetite. In winter, make sure your environment is not excessively hot;
in summer, not excessively cool.

If you live a simple lifestyle and do all things in moderation, the
spirit will be calm, the vital energy will be full, and the generative essence will be strong. When these three energies are plentiful, how can
you not live a healthy and long life?

# 7

## Healthy Diet and Eating Habits

Shen Nong, the herbalist sage, said the following: Those who eat grains will become intelligent and wise, those who ingest minerals and herbs will maintain healthy and youthful bodies, those on a diet of fungi and roots will live a long life, those who swallow the primordial vapor will never be harmed by catastrophes from the sky and disasters from the earth, and those who ingest the pill of the immortals will age with the sky and the earth and last as long as the sun and the moon.

It is said that people who eat a lot of meat will develop ferocity and bravery but will have a short life span. This is why it is natural for warriors to live primarily on a diet of meat. It is also why tribes that are meat eaters tend to be warlike. Those who subsist on a diet of grain tend to be quick-witted and intelligent. They will live longer than meat eaters but not as long as those who eat a diet of vegetables, fungi, and fruit. A vegan diet can help you develop an uncluttered mind and a peaceful disposition, but it will not give you enough strength to engage in work that is physically challenging. Those who live on a diet of vapor and dew will not be subject to illness and aging. Their bodies are light and unencumbered, and they can float with the clouds and ride on the wind.

What is the best kind of diet for cultivating body and spirit? At first, don't let the mind dictate what you should be eat. Dissolve your thoughts through meditation and strengthen the body with *qigong*. When the body has become healthy and the thoughts have become clear, you should eat a balanced diet of meat, vegetables, grains, fungi, and fruit in moderation. At this stage of spiritual development, it is appropriate to maintain a balance of courage, intelligence, and peacefulness. As your practice deepens, your diet will change naturally to optimize the circulation and storage of internal energy. Thus, you may find yourself eating more meat when your physical energy is taxed, more grains when your mental energy is spent, and more vegetables and fruits when you are less active physically and mentally. Finally, you may find yourself not eating at all when you are in a meditative retreat.

The important thing to understand about diet and eating habits is that food is the foundation of health as well as the primary cause of illness. What we eat and how we eat affect both physical health and mental clarity. Generally, it is advisable not to overeat. Stop eating before you feel full. Overeating can cause thoughts to wander, make the body lethargic, and slow the circulation of energy. Sluggish circulation of energy can lead to blockages in the meridians and restrict the flow of nutrients to the internal organs. The deprivation of internal nourishment can have serious consequences on health and longevity.

If you take herbs that enhance health, but you do not live a healthy lifestyle, the herbs won't be very effective. The key to health lies in not eating too much, not going to sleep immediately after a meal, and not sitting around all day without moving. These kinds of habits must be avoided if you want to be healthy. Engage in physical activity frequently but do not tire yourself. Do not exercise rigorously immediately after eating. After a normal meal, walk a mile. After a banquet, walk two miles. After a long walk, massage your legs and feet before sitting down—your body will feel energized and your spirit will be clear.

Do not eat snacks or drink excessively after meals, especially in the evening. Otherwise, undigested food and the effects of the intoxicants will remain in the body while you are asleep, and health problems associated with the stomach and liver will arise.

It is better to eat too little than to overeat. Those who understand how to nourish the body and clear the spirit will eat before they feel famished and will stop eating before they feel full. They will drink liquids before they are thirsty and will stop drinking before their thirst is quenched. If you eat only when you feel hunger, you're bound to eat more than what is enough. If you stop eating only when you feel full, you've probably eaten too much. In general, if you use moderation when you eat and get into the habit of taking a stroll after meals, you'll have a healthy digestive system.

During meals, do not eat steaming hot food after chilled food, and vice versa. The difference in the food temperature will damage the esophagus and the stomach. Do not try to cool your mouth with a cold liquid after eating spicy foods. Use a warm liquid to ease the discomfort. If you feel sick after eating spicy food, it is best that you don't eat it at all. Food that is too spicy can not only damage the internal organs but also weaken the bones and joints. Food that is too chilled can harm the teeth and the five viscera.

When you eat, do nothing but eat. If you eat and work at the same time, blood will be driven up to the head instead of to the stomach and intestines, thereby causing indigestion. If you wish to consume alcohol, drink it with food in the stomach. If you drink on an empty stomach, the normal functioning of the digestive system will be disrupted.

Good eating habits are not difficult to adopt. If you are able to follow them, you'll live a healthy life. Furthermore, if you are able to supplement your diet with the appropriate herbs and the practice of *qigong*, your health and longevity will be much more enhanced.

In spring it is appropriate to eat spicy foods, in summer sour foods, in autumn bitter foods, and in winter salty foods.* Foods with these flavors, when eaten in the appropriate season and in moderation, can strengthen the internal organs and enhance the circulation of blood. If you eat the internal organs of animals, you should refrain from eating the liver in spring, the heart in summer, the lungs in autumn, and the kidneys in winter. You should refrain from eating the spleen in all four seasons. However, it is best if you don't eat the internal organs of animals at all.

If you sleep immediately after a heavy meal, you'll develop back pain. If you ingest too much alcohol, you'll be susceptible to chills and pneumonia. Don't eat too much after drinking a lot of alcohol. It is also good to have some food in the stomach before you drink. Having sex

---

* The implication is that sweet foods can be eaten year-round but not in excess.

after drinking too much will harm the liver, block the circulation of blood, and weaken the bones. In general, it is healthier to eat cooked meat than raw meat. In summer, you can eat cold meat but not raw meat. In winter, eat only warm or cooked food.

The sages say the following: Those who eat a lot of rare meat will tend to be competitive, aggressive, and intolerant. Those who eat a balanced diet of grains, vegetables, and meat will tend to be gentler and kinder and live a more contented life. Although their countenances will be more peaceful, they will still not be completely free from worry and desire. Those who refrain from eating grains and meat and eat only fruits and vegetables will not only have a peaceful countenance but will also live a long and healthy life. Those who are able to circulate the internal energy, still their thoughts, and hold the spirit within will become immortal.

# 8

## Healthy Sexual Lifestyle

If you value health and longevity, you will need to conserve generative energy and pay attention to your sexual habits. Three principles summarize the Taoist approach to cultivating generative energy.

First, sexual interaction is an integral part of human activity that cannot be denied or suppressed. If sexuality is suppressed, desire will increase. When desire increases, the spirit will be preoccupied with sexual fantasies and not be still. If the spirit is not still, life energy will dissipate.

Second, given that sexual arousal and interaction are part of our lives, we need to learn how not to waste generative energy when we are sexually active. Procreative energy is like fire and water. Just as fire can warm or burn us and water can sustain or drown us, sexual energy can create a life or destroy one. If we know how to conserve generative energy, we will be able to enhance our health and lengthen our lives. If we don't know how to conserve it, we will age and die before our time.

Third, sexual activity can damage the body. There are three categories of conditions under which this can happen.

The first relates to climate. It is harmful to engage in sexual activity when it is excessively cold, hot, windy, rainy, or snowy; during earthquakes, eclipses, or thunderstorms; and on the equinoxes and solstices. Having sex during these times will disrupt the harmony of heaven.

The second set of conditions concerns one's internal state. It is harmful to have sex when one is drunk, when the stomach is full, or when one is sad, elated, fearful, or angry. Having sex in these conditions will disrupt the harmony of humanity. Moreover, when these intense emotional states concur with sexual activity, life energy will dissipate more than normal.

The third set of conditions involves location. It is harmful to engage in sexual activity on high mountains, in deep valleys, in sacred places of worship and devotion, and where the guardians of the land reside. Having sex in these places will disrupt the harmony of the earth.

Generative essence is a precious treasure. Used appropriately, it can create another life and improve the quality of a couple's relationship. Conserve it properly, and it will enhance health and lengthen life. Most people find it difficult to be celibate naturally, or they wish to have descendants. Many do not understand that excessive sexual activity can drain the energy of life and lead to premature aging and death. They let desire and possessiveness rule their lives, ejecting the precious life force without knowledge that this act will weaken their bodies. In the natural world, plants and animals procreate according to the cycle of yin and yang and renew themselves naturally with the seasons. If humans can understand the principles of yin and yang, the workings of the earth and the sky, and the waxing and waning cycle of generative energy in our bodies, they will be able to live with their sexual urges naturally while conserving and replenishing generative energy.

If you cannot sleep in the same bed as your partner without being sexually aroused, try sleeping in a different room, in separate beds in the same room, or even in the same bed but without sharing the same blanket. Intense sexual desire can harm the eyesight. Loud and dissonant music can harm the sense of hearing. Too much physical activity can tire the body. Excessive intake of alcohol and rich foods can damage the internal organs. Just as moderation in eating, drinking, and physical and mental activity can enhance health, so it is with sexual activity. Knowing when to have sex, how to conserve energy while having sex, and how to replenish generative energy after having sex can have a significant effect on health.

It is said that the greatest habitual problems are: eating too much daily, getting drunk weekly, and having sex every night.

Should we avoid sexual contact after the age of sixty to conserve the dwindling generative energy? No, said Peng Zu the immortal. It is natural that yin and yang are attracted to each other. If we suppress our sexual urges, or if we force ourselves to avoid sexual contact, desire will increase instead of decrease. The more we suppress sexual desire, the more we will be preoccupied with it. When our thoughts are preoccupied with sex, generative energy will be drained from the body, and the life span will be diminished. Moreover, even if you can suppress sexual urges during waking hours, you won't be able to suppress them during sleep. Consequently, men who force celibacy on themselves often end up ejecting the precious generative essence while sleeping.

When the level of generative energy is low, we become ill. When generative energy is completely dissipated, we die. It is advisable, however, for a man to eject seminal fluid once a week or so. This allows the generative energy in his body to regenerate. But if seminal fluid is ejected several times a day or even once a day, he will lose more energy than he can regenerate.

If we can replenish what was lost, we will live out our natural life span in good health. If we lose more generative energy than we can replenish, we will die prematurely. If we are able to replenish more than what we have lost, we will live beyond the expected normal life span.

In order for generative energy to accumulate, the rate of its generation must exceed its rate of loss. If you can limit sexual activity to twice a month, a tremendous amount of generative energy can be accumulated, and this energy can be used to build bone marrow and strengthen the blood. This is true for both men and women. If a woman can limit herself to having one orgasm twice a month, her blood will be strong and her bones will not degenerate.

Those who let their sexual desire run wild will bring ruin to their bodies. Fantasized sex can lead to the loss of generative energy just as much as physical sexual activity. Paradoxically, sexual desire increases as the level of generative energy diminishes. If generative energy is plentiful, sexual urges actually lessen. When the level of generative energy is low, the body will become gaunt, the complexion will darken, the skin will lose its shininess, the tendons will tighten, and the face will take on a skeletal look. This is because generative energy is integral to the generation of blood and marrow. Without sufficient generative energy, the bones, tendons, and muscles will wither. When the skeletal system weakens, physical movement will become a burden. When physical movement is limited, the circulation of blood will be sluggish. When circulation is sluggish, nutrients will not reach the internal organs effectively and toxins will not be flushed out properly. Eventually, the body will succumb to illness and die.

If sexual activity can be so detrimental to health, one might think that we should abstain from it completely. However, forcing ourselves to abstain from sexual activity can be just as harmful as indulging in it because forced abstinence can increase sexual desire. And when this desire cannot be satisfied, the generative energy can become stagnant. Forced celibacy can lead to abnormal and harmful sexual behavior, mental instability, and a shortening of the life span. The key to having a healthy sexual life lies in regulation and moderation. Initially, discipline is required, but once the level of generative energy is high, regulation becomes natural.

Those who practice the arts of health and longevity should take care not to dissipate generative energy. In general, if you are able to limit the release of generative energy to twice a month, you'll live a healthy and long life. If you are unable to regulate sexual activity to twice a month, then it is advisable to follow these guidelines: in spring and autumn, limit intercourse to once every three days; in summer, once a day; and in winter, abstain completely.

Winter is the time for regeneration. If we dissipate generative energy during the time of regeneration, the accumulated energy cannot be stored properly. Spring is the time for the awakening of energy. If too much generative energy is spent at this time, the reserves stored in winter will be spent rapidly, and there will be little left until the next period of regeneration. Summer is the time we can afford to expend generative energy, but even then we should limit sexual intercourse to once a day. Autumn is the time for the level of generative energy to be low after an active sexual life in the summer; conservation is therefore necessary in autumn.

Most people lose a lot of generative energy when they're young. This is because they do not feel the loss, or they don't understand the need to conserve generative energy when they are strong and youthful. Only when they become old and weak do they realize they should have conserved generative energy early in life. Ideally, we should embark on the path to health and longevity when we're young. The sooner we conserve generative energy, the healthier we will be and the longer we will live. However, this does not mean that it's too late to start conserving and accumulating generative energy after middle age; it only means that the older we are, the more we'll need to practice *qigong* techniques that are designed to restore and accumulate generative energy.

The key to living a healthy and long life is this. Understand that the spirit is the ruler of the body, vital energy is the imperial envoy, the generative essence is the army, the internal and sense organs are the ministers, and the muscles, joints, and tendons are the citizens. When desire dominates, the ruler's directives carried by the envoy will not be followed. The sense organs will indulge in pleasure, the internal organs will refuse to store energy, the generative essence will be spent in useless conquests, and the muscular system will be taxed beyond its capacity. With time, the resources in the nation (the body) will be exhausted. When the resources are depleted, the army will be unable to ward off foreign invaders, the ministers will be corrupt and incompetent, the imperial envoy will no longer be respected, and the true ruler's seat will be usurped by a dictator who delights only in desire and aggression. Those who practice the arts of longevity must understand that the fall of the body-nation begins with desire and self-indulgence. They must realize that cultivating the life force begins and ends with calming the spirit, cultivating contentment, and leading a life of moderation.

## PART THREE

# The Taoist in Private Life

## The Art of Concealment: Hidden Sky

Teachings from *The Great Patriarch Laozi's Treatise on Internal Awareness*, *The Great Mysterious Grotto Precious Classic on the Subtle Method of Turning Awareness Inward*, and *The Nine Cultivations*

# 9

# Turning Awareness Inward

When the yin and yang vapors of the earth and the sky interact, these two energies will swirl to create the ten thousand things. When male and female copulate, the luminous spark of life of the Tao, along with karmic connections from past lives, will emerge in the womb of the mother as a fetus.

In the first month of conception, the essence of the blood crystalizes to form the membrane that encloses the embryo. In the second month, the embryo is transformed and begins to take on the form of a fetus. In the third month, the three souls (*hun*) emerge from the primordial yang spirit and begin to stir. In the fourth month, the seven soul-spirits (*po*) emerge from the primordial yin spirit to stabilize the bodily form. In the fifth month, the five elements manifest as the five viscera (fire as the heart, wood as the liver, earth as the spleen, metal as the lungs, and water as the kidneys) to support the yang spirit. In the sixth month, the six bowels (bladder, gall bladder, stomach, large intestine, small intestine, and the triple heater meridian) begin to form, to support and nourish the yin spirit. In the seventh month, the generative essence thrusts through the cavities, opening the seven orifices of the head to communicate with light. In the eighth month, the eight guardian spirits of each of the three regions (head, chest, and abdomen), or palaces, of the body are fully formed, and the true spirit enters the body of the fetus. In the ninth month, all the palaces in the body are adorned and readied to host the guardian spirits. In the tenth month, the life energy in the fetus reaches its height, and the infant is ready to be born.

After the infant is born, its breath interchanges continuously with the primordial vapor of the sky and the earth. The guardian deity of the upper palace (upper *dantian*, or energy center) takes its seat in the Mudball cavity and rules over all the other guardian deities. It gives birth to the knowledge-spirit and is merged with the soul. The guardian deity of vitality establishes itself in the middle palace (middle *dantian*) and is responsible for connecting the body to the source of life energy. Other guardian deities emerge to rule the three souls (*hun*) and the seven soul-spirits (*po*), to protect the life gate (which is the root of generative energy), and to nourish the joints, muscles, and bones. Within the body are numerous guardian spirits, great and small, to ensure that the energy of life is secured within.

At birth, the primordial vapors of the sky and the earth enter our bodies through the nostrils. From there it flows to the Mudball cavity. When this vapor enters the Mudball cavity, the spirit will be clear and luminous and the body will be restful and relaxed. Actions and thoughts are ruled by the spirit. If the spirit is clear, thoughts will be wise and actions will be decisive. If the spirit is distracted, thoughts will be muddy and actions will be hesitant. The key to knowing whether the spirit is clear or distracted is to orient our awareness within.

The spirit (*shen*) has the ability to moderate thoughts and actions. When it is allowed to rule properly, it can regulate mental, physical, and energetic activities and prevent thoughts and behavior from going awry. The spirit moves in subtle, mysterious, and profound ways and cannot be grasped by conceptual thinking.

Each of the five viscera is ruled by a guardian spirit. The liver is the home of the guardian of the soul, the lungs are the home of the soul-spirit, the kidneys are the home of the generative essence, the spleen is the home of aspiration, and the heart is the home of the spirit. Within the scheme of the five elements, the heart belongs to the element fire and is ruled by the essence of the sun. The energetic structure of the heart is shaped like a three-petaled lotus, and its manifestations are ephemeral and numerous.

A manifestation can take on hues of green, white, charcoal, and yellow. It is neither large nor small, short nor long, crooked nor straight, soft nor hard, thick nor thin, circular nor square. Because it is intangible, its transformations are limitless and its power profound. It can merge with yin and yang, embrace the sky and the earth, or hide in a pore in the body. When the heart rules properly, our mental, physical, and energetic behaviors will be harmonious. When the heart does not rule properly, thoughts will be extreme, physical activity will tend to be violent, bodily functions will be disrupted, and the energy of life will dissipate.

If the spirit is clear and still, we will live long and healthy lives. A spirit that is distracted and aggressive will lead to early illness and death. A spirit that is bright and luminous will radiate wisdom and compassion. A spirit that is dull and dim will bring confusion, fear, and doubt. If we can let the spirit rest in stillness, our lives will be long and healthy. If the spirit dwells in relaxed effortlessness, body and consciousness will be harmonious. Although the spirit is formless and intangible, it is nonetheless responsible for our fortune and our misfortune. If the spirit is bright and clear, our thoughts and actions will attract auspiciousness. If the spirit is wayward and violent, our thoughts and actions will bring misfortune.

The sages understood that the prosperity and well-being of a nation are dependent on the principles of rulership. They laid down the proper relationship among ruler, minister, and citizen. Governance was established to regulate political, social, and economic activity, and laws were passed to ensure justice. The body is like a nation, and the principles of rulership apply similarly. If the ruler (the spirit) is wayward, the ministers (the guardian spirits of the regions of the body) will waste energy and not function harmoniously.

Physical and mental health begin with stilling the spirit. If the spirit is pure and clear, actions will be peaceful, and there will no room for hatred and aggression to emerge. If there is no hatred and aggression in our thoughts and actions, there will be no residue of these destructive energies when we pass away naturally. As a result, our future lifetimes will not be tainted by tendencies toward anger and violence.

Our lives are miserable when the spirit is clouded by desire, negative emotions, and confusion. Desire generates anxiety about gain and loss; negative emotions generate anger, violence, and aggression; and confusion leads to fear and doubt. These negative energies tie us in knots, spinning us deeper and deeper into further doubt, aggression, and anxiety. Consequently, we are unable to respond to reason, clarity, and wisdom. Like stubborn mules, we walk into the quagmire of confusion and are trapped there until we die.

When we are born, the spirit is naturally clear and still. As we come into contact with the social, political, and economic environment, the spirit is captured by social and peer pressure, thoughts are confused by political ideologies, and the senses are captured by material things. Sights that please the eye, sounds and speech that please the faculty of hearing, taste that pleases the palate, praise that pleases our pride, and fame that pleases our vanity—all these begin to take root in the spirit, pulling it down into the muck of desire and confusion. The sages, seeing the suffering of humanity, devised methods of help us see the roots of desire and confusion. One of these methods is the meditative technique of tuning our awareness within.

Observe the structure and functions of the body, and you will understand that it emerges from the Great Void. When the conditions of life are met, the generative essences copulate, the spirit enters the womb, and the primordial vapors (of yin and yang) harmonize to create a fetus. Our bodies are patterned after the laws of the universe: we inhale and exhale the breath of yin and yang, the five elements (the internal organs) within us interact, and the rise and fall of our energies follow the cycle of the seasons. The eyes are the sun and the moon, the hair is the stars, the eyebrows are the clouds, and the head is Mount Kunlun. Palaces, courts, and pavilions are arrayed throughout the body to house the guardian spirits.

It is said that humans have the greatest potential to realize the Tao within. The human body and spirit are naturally in harmony with the Tao. Observe the subtleties of the body, and you will see the treasures stored within. Yet we humans are ignorant of the precious essences we are endowed with. As we are drawn into the dust of the materialistic world, toxins pervade our bodies, and the spirit becomes wayward and mad. If we scrutinize the phenomena of the natural world and the activity of our internal universe, we will realize that their cycles of activity and stillness follow the same principles. If we want to cultivate health and longevity, we need to hold the Tao within, do meritorious deeds, and let our original nature shine. Those who go after material, political, and social gains will only tire body and spirit and bring worry and anxiety into their lives.

The spark of existence that humans receive from the Tao is called life. That which we receive from the natural way is called original nature. That which commands our activity is consciousness. When thoughts arise in consciousness, this is intention. Intention that is directed to objects in the world is called aspiration. The ability to discriminate and make decisions rationally is called intelligence. When intelligence intuits the nature of things, it is wisdom. That which pervades the body and protects its form is the soul. That which abides in stillness to stabilize the form is the soul-spirit. That which flows through the flesh and bones is the blood. That which nourishes the spirit and primordial life force is the generative essence. The primordial life force that is light and that rises is the minister. The primordial life force that is heavy and that sinks is the guard. That which holds together the skeletal system and the internal organs is the body. That which gives the body its form and shape is substance. That which can fathom the depth of things is the spirit. When the spirit is subtle and unfixed, we call it luminous. When the spirit is luminous, life energy is strong. When luminosity leaves the body, we die.

That which gives us life is the Tao. The Tao is formless and has no structure. Yet it resonates with all things. Its transformations are limitless and can nourish and make all things grow. Within us, the Tao manifests as original nature. Therefore, to cultivate original nature is to cultivate the Tao. Because the Tao is without form, its functions can be intuited only by observing its manifestations in body and spirit. We cannot lengthen our lives except by allowing the Tao to guide us. Death is the exhaustion of the Tao within. However, if we are able to unite our life force with the Tao, we will live a long and healthy life. Humans suffer from illness and early death because they don't know how to turn their awareness within to see this unity. Therefore, if we are to attain longevity and well-being, the technique of internal gazing must be practiced diligently.

People wander around in confusion, get stuck in nonvirtuous ways, and find themselves trapped in the murky grounds of ignorance because of desire. From desire comes attachment. Attachment affects our senses, conceptualizing everything in the environment as attractive or not attractive. Consequently, we swing wildly between moods of extreme love and hate. Imprisoned by worry and anxiety, we stray farther and farther away from the Tao.

Attachments come from desire. Desires come from obsessive thinking. When thoughts get out of control, they generate an orientation to likes and dislikes.

The primordial spirit is the Tao within. It is originally and naturally empty and still. If a discursive thought emerges to disturb the natural stillness, attachment to things in the world arises. From attachment come the dualities of gain and loss, attraction and repulsion, favor and disfavor. Once these dualistic thoughts take hold, we are drawn into the web of anxiety and confusion. Caught in the vortex of desire and self-centeredness, we become trapped in the endless cycle of life and death.

The Tao does not know life and death. Only those who have distanced themselves from the Tao are subject to clinging to life and fearing death. That which is formless is not subject to growth and decay. That which has form, however, will endlessly travel the cycle of birth, aging, sickness, and death. Those who understand that they owe their existence to the Tao and who practice the technique of turning their awareness to the Tao within will be able to renew themselves with the life force of the Tao and live peaceful and long lives. If you abide in stillness and maintain clarity, the Tao will naturally stay with you. When the Tao stays within you, the bright and clear spirit will be held within your body. If the bright spirit is held within, you will live a healthy and long life.

Many people wish to live long and healthy lives, but they don't want to still their thoughts. In this way, they're not that different from those who want positions of power and responsibility but are unwilling to use ethical and legitimate ways to attain it, those who want wealth but don't want to work hard to earn it, those who want to arrive at their destinations but are hesitant to move, and those who want to be physically strong but are unwilling to exercise.

The Tao is embraced through cultivating the spirit. Spirit is bright and clear because of the Tao. If the spirit is not drawn into discursiveness, the Tao will naturally stay within. When the Tao stays within, the spirit will be naturally still. The brightness of the spirit is intimately related to the physical health of the body. This relationship is analogous to that of the brightness of a flame and the oil that fuels it. Light arises from the flame, the flame is sustained by the wick, the wick is fed by the oil, and the oil is held by its container. Thus, flame, wick, oil, and container all contribute to the brightness of the light. If any of these four malfunction, there will be no light.

Similarly, the Tao within is related to the brightness of our spirit, the brightness of the spirit is dependent on clarity and stillness, our clarity and stillness are determined by our ability to dissolve wayward thoughts (through meditation), and the ability to dissolve wayward thoughts depends on whether the body has the physical structure to maintain the correct meditative posture. These four—brightness of spirit, clarity and stillness, meditation, and body structure—are all needed for the Tao to dwell within. Lose one of them, and the Tao will leave.

Brightness of spirit means that whatever our eyes can see, whatever our ears can hear, and wherever our aspirations are directed, we are not clouded by ignorance and conceptual bias. It means that we can scrutinize details and yet hold a vast view. All this is possible only when our spirit is bright and our bodies are healthy.

Stillness means dissolving desires and conceptualizations. Desires and conceptualizations are dissolved when consciousness is not being pulled in different directions, when we are not drawn into nonvirtuous thoughts and actions, when there is space for consciousness to expand, when we are not dragged down by the heaviness of discursiveness, and when our thoughts are not tainted by negativity.

Removing the obstacles of stillness involves working on the four states of consciousness. In the first state, consciousness holds its center and is not drawn into confusion by the things happening around us. In the second state, consciousness is balanced and views all things as equal. In the third state, consciousness is bright and has nothing to hide. In the fourth state, consciousness is limitless and is not bound by conceptions. The development of each of these four states of consciousness comes from the practice of turning our awareness within and being tuned to the nature of consciousness.

It is easy to understand the Tao but difficult to believe in it. It is easy to believe in the Tao but difficult to act according to its principles. It is easy to act according to the principles of the Tao but difficult to embrace the Tao. It is easy to embrace the Tao but difficult to stand firm in it. If you can stand firm and hold on to the Tao, you will attain health and longevity.

The teachings of the Tao cannot be transmitted by theory and concepts. If you are able to still your thoughts and maintain peace and simplicity, the Tao will naturally emerge within. Those who are ignorant of the Tao spend their lives tiring the body and pushing their mental capacity beyond their limits, not knowing that as their spirit and life energy are increasingly taxed, they get farther and farther away from the Tao. Even in the pursuit of the Tao, you should not force your progress or see it as an achievement. In doing so, you are already defeating the natural way of cultivating the Tao.

Cultivating the Tao begins with valuing life. We need to nourish our spirit and life energy, stay connected to the source of life, and not let the primordial life force within dissipate. Don't let the natural tendency toward simplicity and stillness be tainted by attraction and repulsion. Merge the spirit and life energy with the Tao. In time, you will attain longevity and immortality. The immortals are those who emerge and dissolve with the sky and the earth, roam the expanse of vastness freely and leisurely, and travel paths unknown to ordinary people. They ingest the vapors of yin and yang, are omniscient, and renew themselves with the eternal turning of the seasons. The world may whirl around them, but they sit in stillness, silently aware of the changes that turn and swirl around them.

The method of turning our awareness within requires us to still our thoughts, maintain a relaxed physical posture, and not be drawn into things that happen around us. Once we are aware that our mental activity has slowed down, we can turn our awareness toward consciousness itself. Externally, the body is relaxed and still; internally, the awareness is sunk deep into the unfathomable depths of vastness. Embrace the subtleties of the action and nonaction of consciousness and intuit the true nature of their arising and dissolution.

Once you have gained insight into the activity and nonactivity of consciousness, clarity will emerge. Abide in this clarity, and purity will emerge. Abide in purity, and the spirit will naturally rest in deep stillness. At this point, spirit and body are merged with the natural rising and falling of life energy. Coming and going, creating and dissolving, and appearing and disappearing without bias, inhaling and exhaling— all become part of the natural way.

# 10

# Heightening Awareness

If you want to understand the subtle mysteries of the Tao, you must first abandon nonvirtuous ways, dissolve your ties to materialism, and not let desire control your life. Next, still your thoughts and relax your body. Slow down mental activity until thoughts cease. With the continued practice of stilling thoughts, you will feel inner peace and harmony.

Those who wish to cultivate the Tao must tame the wayward mind and not be led astray by desire, but they should also not let fixed habits bury the natural way. They need to dissolve mental activity and dwell in stillness, but they should not be attached to emptiness or be obsessive about their practice. Let the natural openness of consciousness emerge and expand. Emptiness without brightness will only stifle the natural way. No matter what happens in the world around you, you must not be dragged toward those matters. Regardless of whether your practice environment is noisy or quiet, you must abide in stillness.

If you are impatient and try to speed up your progress in cultivating the Tao, you can become mentally unstable or even sustain internal injuries. The negative consequences of mispractice can burn you up inside and block the flow of life force within. If you become aware that you are getting dogmatic in your practice, you need to let go, and you may even need to shorten your practice session. Let consciousness settle naturally into stillness. Let thoughts dissolve without force. Be familiar with the arising of various emotions, identify them, and tune into their conditions of arising. When your awareness is tuned into the coming and going of emotions, the stirring of feelings will naturally disappear. Most important, you need to abandon feelings of self-pity when the environment seems obstructive. You also need to abandon the feelings of luck or fortune when your environment is supportive. This is what is meant by settling into natural stillness.

Don't use the excuse of wanting to escape from anxiety and worry to embrace stillness. You should never "want" or "desire" to be still. Stillness is the absence of thoughts. Once thoughts are extinguished, you will naturally be still. Once natural stillness settles within, the natural brightness of wisdom will shine. Do not be impatient with results, and do not be attached to notions of "progress" or "improvement." This will only generate obstacles. Settling into natural stillness cannot be rushed. Nor can it be "made" to happen. It must emerge naturally. Once natural stillness emerges, it must settle deep within. Once wisdom emerges, you must not use it to scheme. Wisdom cannot be "used." It can only be what it naturally is. To "use" wisdom is to lose it. If you are able to let wisdom emerge, settle, and rest naturally within, the barriers you have constructed between you and the Tao will disappear.

To realize the Tao within, practitioners need to cultivate spirit and body simultaneously. To cultivate the spirit, which is the original nature of emptiness, you need to journey through five stages. To cultivate the body, which is the container of the life force, you need to go through seven steps.

In the first of the five stages of cultivating the spirit, you encounter stray thoughts and find it difficult to enter stillness. You are generally preoccupied with a lot of things about the world, yourself, and others. Periods of stillness are short compared to periods of busy mental activity. In the second stage, stillness is less alien to you, and you are able to be comfortable with it as a companion. In this stage, wayward thoughts decrease, and periods of stillness increase. In the third stage, periods of stillness begin to be longer than periods of mental activity. Stray thoughts are dissolved; preoccupation with affairs that affect you personally appears in your thoughts only occasionally. This is a sign that the wayward consciousness has been dissolved and that conceptualizing activity is beginning to take a back seat. However, complete stillness still eludes you.

In the fourth stage of cultivating the spirit, discursiveness is no longer an issue if there are no distractions. However, if emergencies occur in your life, stillness immediately gives way to worry and anxiety. This is a sign that stillness has not taken a firm seat in your practice. In the fifth and final stage, the spirit is no longer separate from the Tao. Regardless of what is happening in your life, your center of stillness is not shaken. The spirit is now bright and clear, and will no longer be tainted with dimness.

In the first of the seven steps of cultivating the body, your body learns to relax and can support consciousness entering stillness. The body no longer feels uncomfortable staying in a sitting posture. In the second step, internal energy begins to circulate without hindrance, and physical and internal injuries are healed. The body now feels good and healthy. In the third step, the three internal energies—generative (*jing*), vital (qi), and spirit (*shen*)—reach healthy levels and penetrate the bones, the meridians, the internal organs, and the *dantian*s. You are storing more energy than you are expending. Your complexion and appearance begin to take on a youthful appearance.

In the fourth step of cultivating the body, your life span is lengthened, and you begin to live as an "earth immortal." In the fifth step, the internal energies return to their pristine form. No toxins remain in the body, and the transmutation of the three energies occurs effortlessly and naturally. At this stage, you have become a "realized being." In the sixth step, the spirit energy can exit and reenter your body at will and travel to other realms. With this, you become omniscient, your actions affecting events throughout space and time. At this stage, you are a "spirit being." In the seventh and final step, the spirit is refined so that it merges with the Tao. You age with the sun and the moon, wander among the stars, rise and ebb with the natural cycles of yin and yang, and move with the elements and the seasons. You have become a "sky immortal."

Those who cultivate the Tao need to traverse the five stages of developing the bright and clear spirit and the seven steps of refining the primal life force. If you progress too fast in cultivating the spirit, the foundations of each stage will not be stable, and you will fall back to the initial stage easily. If you progress too slowly, your discipline must be strengthened. If you develop too fast in cultivating the body, you run the risk of being tempted to use internal energy to feed the ego, which can lead to enhanced aggression and internal bodily injuries. If you develop too slowly, you are still taxing your body beyond its limits, not allowing it to rest properly, or being too lazy in keeping up with your *qigong* practices.

Knowing the five stages and seven steps of cultivating the Tao are key to developing heightened internal awareness. This heightened awareness is important in helping you to monitor your development and in finding appropriate help from adepts to guide your training, if necessary.

# 11

# Turning Awareness Outward

## *Nine Ways of Cultivating the Tao*

### CULTIVATING HARMONY

Before heaven and earth were formed, all things were undifferentiated and united with the Tao. Then the clear and the muddy separated. The clear formed the sky, and the muddy formed the earth. The four seasons came into being, and yin and yang emerged. From the pure essence of the vapor of the Tao, humans were formed. From the mundane energy, insects came into being. As hardness and softness interacted, the world of myriad things proliferated. Essence and spirit belong to heaven. Bones and joints belong to earth. Essence and spirit fly up to the celestial realm, and bones and joints form the roots and foundation beneath.

The sage follows the ways of both heaven and earth. He is neither influenced by social fads nor seduced by conformity. Heaven is his father, earth is his mother, and the principle of yin and yang is his guide. He lives in harmony with the four seasons. His clarity is like the stillness of heaven, and his inner peace is like the stability of earth. Those who stray from the way of the Tao will die, but those who follow it will live. The spirit of those who cultivate stillness is bright, for the Tao lives in minds that are empty and free of desire.

This is why it is said, "The One gives birth to Two, the Two gives birth to Three, and the Three gives birth to the ten thousand myriad things." All things come from the interaction of yin and yang, and the one primordial breath of life always moves toward harmony. Therefore, it is important to cultivate harmony.

## CULTIVATING THE SPIRIT

Humanity owes its existence to transformations in heaven and on earth. The human form is conceived in the first month. In the second month the shell of the fetus emerges. In the third month the skin is formed. In the fourth month the fetus begins to take on a shape. In the fifth month the tendons are formed. In the sixth month the bones begin to grow. In the seventh month the bodily form is complete. In the eighth month the fetus begins to move. In the ninth month it tumbles around in the womb. In the tenth month it is born.

When the baby is born, it possesses the complete form of a human. The five viscera constitute the internal form. The lungs are linked to the nose, the kidneys to the ears, the heart to the tongue, and the liver to the eyes.* We are identified by our external features, but the real identity lies within. The head is round like the sky. The feet plant squarely on the ground like the earth. Just as the universe has 4 seasons, 5 elements, and 9 stars,† and the year has 360 days, humans have 4 limbs, 5 viscera, 9 orifices, and 360 joints.

In nature we find wind, rain, cold, and heat. In humans we find happiness and anger. The gall bladder is the clouds, the lungs are the vapor, the spleen is the wind, the kidneys are the lightning, and the liver is the thunder. The human body mirrors the macrocosm of heaven and earth. In humans, the heart directs all activities. The eyes and the ears are the sun and the moon. The blood and the generative energy are the wind and the rain. When the sun and the moon deviate from their orbits, light will vanish, and there will be eclipses. When wind and rain do not come at the appropriate time, there will be disasters. When the five elements do not follow their cycle of creation, all living things will suffer.

Heaven and earth are great and can nourish all things. However,

---

* The fifth viscus, the spleen, is not mentioned in the original text. In traditional Chinese medicine the spleen is the unifier of the other four viscera; it is not linked to the sense of touch.

† The seven stars of the Big Dipper, plus two adjacent stars.

they need to maintain their balance by not overextending their energy. In the same way, our eyes and ears cannot work without rest. We cannot expect our generative energy and spirit to remain strong if we do not conserve them. The sage knows the value of life and therefore cultivates the spirit in order not to lose the essence and energy of life.

## CULTIVATING THE ENERGY

The energy in the blood is the essence of life, and the five viscera are containers holding this essence. When the energy in the blood is secure within and does not leak out, the heart is open and desires are at a minimum. When desires are minimal, the eyes can see clearly and the ears can hear clearly. When the five viscera are in harmony with the heart, awareness is clear and not cluttered. You will be able to listen and hear everything and to look and see everything. No harm will come to you, for the bad vapors will not be able to penetrate you. However, if you ask too much, you will get little; if you try to see too much, you will end up knowing little.

Generative energy and spirit are lost through the orifices of the body. Vital energy and intention follow the five viscera. When the ears and the eyes are attracted by sound and sight, the five viscera will be shaken, energy in the blood will be churned up, and the spirit will sway and not be focused.

Fortune and misfortune are not always accidental. The sage knows how to avoid them. She is dedicated to clearing her ears and eyes of attachments so that she will not be enticed. Her emotions are tamed, her disposition is peaceful, and she has few desires. Internally, the five viscera function properly. Her spirit is gathered, and her body is not strained by physical exertion. Her gaze is directed away from worldly affairs, and she responds only to what affects her immediately.

Those who are greedy for knowledge end up learning the least. The spirit should not roam far. Otherwise, desires will arise. With the arousal of desire, the five colors will confuse the eyes and obstruct seeing. The five notes of the Chinese pentatonic scale will enter the ears and obstruct hearing. The five flavors will confuse the tongue and obstruct the sense of taste. When the consciousness is scattered, original nature will stray. If you have too many desires, the breath of life will be weak. If there is too much hatred, the heart will be strained. People do not live out their full years because they are too attached to material things. Only those who can live in emptiness and inaction can attain health and longevity.

The ways of heaven and earth follow natural cycles. All things in heaven and on earth come from the Tao. If you know the Tao, there is nothing that you will not know. If you don't know the Tao, you will know nothing. The Tao, which is the One, leads to the Two. When two things interact, another entity is born. Therefore, life is not a big event, and death is not the end of all things. You should not be repulsed by ugliness and attracted to the precious. Know your limit and be at peace with it. Do not revel in extremes, or you will lose happiness easily.

Fluctuations of sadness and happiness destroy virtue. Hatred tires the heart. Attraction and desire are deviations from the Tao. Life comes from the movement of heaven, and death comes with decay and dissolution. In stillness, you should be in union with yin and virtue. In action, you should be in tune with yang and movement. Consciousness is never separated from the body. Spiritual energy is the treasure of consciousness. When the body labors too much, it becomes injured. When you think too much, the spirit becomes exhausted.

The sage lives in accordance with the times and is satisfied with his place in the world. He responds to activity in emptiness; therefore, he can see far and understand the rationale of things. He uses emptiness to hold the full, understands moderation, and is quiet in his speech. Thus, he lives his life to its fullest. Nothing bothers him because he is attached to nothing. He embraces virtue, cultivates harmony, follows the way of heaven, and is in stride with the Tao. He does not place fortune or calamity first because he knows that the matters of life and death do not alter his existence. His spirit guides his actions; therefore, whatever he does, he succeeds.

## CULTIVATING RIGHT ACTION

If you don't place a lot of importance on worldly matters, your spirit will not be tired. If you don't think too much about material things, you will not be confused. If you can let go of life and death, your intention will not be led astray. If you can merge with changes in heaven and on earth, your clarity will not be diminished.

The enlightened ones stand firm whether or not they are supported by others. Because they learn from teachers who are timeless, they can penetrate and understand everything. Knowing how to yield and bend, they can hold their lives in their hands and survive under any condition. Transforming misfortune into fortune, they are free from the bonds of gain and loss. Their integrity cannot be shaken by force or threats of violence.

If you follow the path of right action, you will not be afraid of death; if you understand nonaction, you will be free from anxiety; and if you are without anxiety, you can embrace the world with an open heart. Listen to the advice of the enlightened ones, for they teach you the meaning of right action. Use gratitude as your guide, and you will have enough to live in the world.

## CULTIVATING CONTENTMENT

Desire for wealth and power is natural for most people. However, this makes their bodies sick. The sage, however, is content to eat enough to circulate energy and wear enough to keep warm. She does not indulge in emotions or accumulate possessions. Because her eyes are pure, she does not desire to see. Because her ears are still, she does not want to hear. She closes her mouth and refrains from talking; she quiets her mind and refrains from thinking. Abandoning sharp intelligence to return to oneness, she rests her spirit and lets go of knowledge. Thus, there is nothing for her to love or hate. Having penetrated the mystery of everything, she dispenses with worry and anxiety. Because she is rooted in the Source, there is nothing that she cannot do.

Those who know how to live harmoniously are not attracted by gain and reward. Those who have broken the barrier between the internal and the external will not be tempted by power. The sages respect the macrocosm of the universe and value the microcosm of the body. Knowing the great value of life, they can go anywhere without hindrance.

## CULTIVATING SIMPLICITY

The ancient sages knew how to regulate thoughts and emotions, tame the will and intentions, cultivate inner harmony, and live simply. If you delight in the Tao, you will forget social gains. Cultivate virtue, and you will forget desire. Minimize desire, and you will not be distracted by pleasure or be affected by happiness and sadness. If you are moody and sentimental, however, you will lose your virtue. If you are liberal with emotional outbursts, you will find it hard to be harmonious. Know how to tame your intentions and live in moderation, and you will be an example to humanity.

Eat only what is necessary. Wear only what is sufficient. Live simply and travel modestly. Do not be extreme in your actions. Do not desire to have all the things in the world. Do not harm others to benefit yourself. Why let the concerns of riches and poverty, gain and loss, ruin your physical health and mental well-being? Know this, and you will understand the Tao.

## CULTIVATING CLARITY

Humanity owes its existence to the Tao. The ears and the eyes attend to sounds and sights, the nose discriminates the fragrant from the pungent, and the skin senses the difference between heat and cold. The difference between a sage and a mundane person is in the rise and fall of the individual's feelings and emotions. The spirit is the source of knowing. When the spirit is clear, we know intuitively. When we understand the difference between the private and the public, we are at peace with ourselves. Human consciousness is like a river. Just as clear water is still, intention is still when the spirit is clear. If the spirit is clear, attachments to things in the world do not arise.

Strong intentions disturb clarity. Only those whose consciousness is clear will not be affected by worldly concerns and material gains. Only those whose spirit is clear will not be bothered by desires and will be able to sleep peacefully. If our consciousness is directed outward to things, the spirit will follow. However, if it is empty of desire, attachments will dissolve naturally. This is the way of the sage. Therefore, if you want to help others, you must tame your emotions first.

The sage does not let his emotions run wild. He eats only enough to fill his belly and wears only enough to keep warm. Content to live simply, he has no desires. To possess the world, you must not wish to possess anything. To be respected, you must not be concerned about being famous. Be honest with yourself and exercise virtue and integrity. If the spirit is clear and there are no desires and attachments, you will not be bothered by anything. Gain and loss will have no effect on you. Sights and sounds will not distract you. Arguments will not convince you, opinions will not sway you, and force will not frighten you. This is the way of the sage.

That which gives birth to life does not die, and that which dissolves things does not disintegrate. That which rules heaven and earth, which gives light to the sun and the moon, which affects the cycles of change, and which gives birth to rocks and metals does not favor anything in particular. The sage knows all this and therefore does not waver in cultivation.

With stillness comes nonattachment. This is why in stillness we can cultivate life. Harmony, friendliness, and lack of self-interest can help you to be virtuous. When the events of the world do not distract you, you will be at peace. When there is stillness within, you will be content with your place in the world. In contentment, you can cultivate health and longevity and hold on to virtue all your life. If you do not attain stillness, however, then the circulation of blood will be blocked, the internal organs will not be able to store energy, and you will be plagued with anxiety and worry. Anxious about social gains and loss, you will tire both body and spirit.

Today, many are concerned with worldly matters. Some complain about their troubles. Others bemoan the fact that they cannot escape from misfortune. Those who see only the end of autumn will not hear the sound of thunder. Those who hear only the jingle of gold will fail to see the grandeur of the mountains. If you are too attached to little things, you will miss the important ones.

Things in the world can distract our minds and arouse our emotions. Generative energy dissipates when there are desires. In a clear pool, mud settles at the bottom. However, it takes only a small ripple to churn up the mud and destroy the stillness. Consciousness is like a pool of water. It is easy to be stirred up by events in the world, but it is difficult to be clear and still.

The way of heaven is the sacred way. Below it is the way of scholars, and at the bottom is the way of politicians. If politicians rule, the natural way is in danger. If scholars rule, we will see the beginning of trouble. If the way of heaven rules, the principles of stillness and emptiness will be followed. In emptiness everything will be taken care of, and in stillness nothing will be left out. Know the way of emptiness and stillness, and you will understand the beginning and the end of all things. The enlightened person sees stillness as order and movement as chaos. If things are left alone, everything will run its course. In the absence of fear, threat, and force, all things will function naturally. This is the way of heaven.

## CULTIVATING HUMILITY

Rulers view their country as theirs to own, and they are proud of their possessions. The powerful ones use their armies to conquer; the weaker ones are forced to submit. Display of wealth and power is the norm for most people. However, just as the fierce storms of summer are short-lived, so are political power and armed force.

Understanding this, the sage lives in accordance with the Tao, abides in nonaction, and keeps her energy in harmony and balance. She cultivates humility and softness and abstains from the use of force. She is like the great rivers and seas, silently gathering waters from a hundred streams and springs. This is why her wisdom is great and her virtue is limitless.

The sage wins respect through humility; therefore, he can become a natural ruler. He values the feminine; therefore, he can live forever. He reveres life; therefore, he is noble and honorable. He is awed by the powers of nature; therefore, he places everything above himself. He understands the meaning of responsibility; therefore, he knows that lack of seriousness will not get tasks accomplished.

It is natural that the great comes from the small and the many are accumulated from the few. Therefore, the sage follows the way of the Tao and acts in humility. She does not despise things that are lowly or incomplete. She values simplicity, holds on to the principle of smallness, and practices nonaction. Because she realizes that she is incomplete, she can be virtuous. Because she is yielding, she can adapt to different conditions.

Those who are rigid will not last long, those who are strong will die, and those who are satisfied with themselves will perish. Strong winds and heavy rains do not last because their energy is spent quickly. Small and narrow valleys escape the storms because they are not exposed. Knowing these principles, the sage holds on to the feminine and does not display power and strength. Because he has the softness of the female, he has the strength of the male. He does not crave power and greatness; therefore, he will live long.

Fullness and emptiness follow each other in the natural world. When fullness reaches its height, waning begins, and when emptiness is attained, waxing begins. The sage maintains harmony and is not proud or greedy. Each day she follows the path of the feminine, making sure that her virtue does not diminish.

The mundane person, however, tends to bow to those in power and dismiss those without status. He admires the intelligent and despises the dull-witted. He wants reward and hates punishment. He gravitates toward the socially prestigious and avoids those who are nameless. People who have these tendencies will not attain the Tao.

The sage follows the way of heaven. She accomplishes by doing nothing and gathers by not grabbing. She feels the same way as the ordinary person but follows a different path. That is why she can live long.

The sagely rulers of ancient times did not indulge in extremes. They knew that when something reaches its height, it will begin to wane. When it is full, it will begin to diminish. When things reach their greatest strength, they will decay. Just as the sun must set after it reaches the highest point in the sky, and the moon must wane after it becomes full, happiness and excitement must be followed by sadness and boredom. The wise person should therefore hold on to simplicity, the learned person to humility, the strong person to carefulness, the rich person to contentment, and the virtuous person to selflessness. The ancient rulers were respected by all because they followed these principles and did not crave completeness and absolute mastery. If you cannot cultivate humility, you will lose sight of the Tao and fall into decay.

## CULTIVATING SOFTNESS

The sage rests with the yin and rises with the yang. Because he has transcended happiness and sadness, he is content and joyful at all times. His joy comes from the depths of his spirit, although he does not show it externally. Because he is joyful inside, he does not see himself through the eyes of others. He cultivates stillness and clarity because he knows that craving and hating come from thoughts and desires. The sage does not experience excitement, anger, happiness, and pain because he is at one with all things and is beyond truth and falsehood.

When people know how to conduct themselves, they will be respected naturally. They won't need money to be wealthy, and they won't need to be forceful to be strong. They will not desire material goods, want fame and fortune, or be concerned with recognition and prestige. When wants and desire are absent, body, spirit, and energy will not fail.

The body is the vessel of life. Energy is its root, and spirit is the regulator. If either the body or the spirit loses its function, the other will be injured. If the spirit dominates and becomes the root, the body will crave. If the body tries to lead, the spirit will be harmed. Pride, desire, and fame drain energy; a dominating intelligence injures the spirit; and sexual pleasure destroys the body. If we are blinded by ignorance, we will harm the body, energy, and spirit. With time, illness will take hold of the body, and feebleness will take hold of consciousness.

Body, energy, and spirit renew themselves in stillness. If you are irritable, you will lose the three essences of life (generative energy, vital energy, and spirit energy) and become old. The sage therefore cultivates the spirit, harmonizes the energy, and regulates sensations. Rising and falling with the breath of the Tao, she merges with everything. Abiding in stillness, she is not disturbed by events happening around her.

Sages have nothing but possess all. They appear empty but are filled. They cultivate the internals and are not concerned with the externals. They embrace softness and return to simplicity. They hold on to the spirit and travel the expanse of heaven and earth. Removed from the dust of the world, they live in leisure and freedom. They are attuned to everything but are not attached to anything. True to themselves, they do not compete with the world. They see changes but hold on to the permanent. Their intention is contained within, and they are always in touch with oneness. They understand without reasoning, see without looking, accomplish without doing, distinguish without discriminating, feel without responding, and resort to action only out of necessity.

Sages are like a light that does not dazzle and a scene that is not busy. They model themselves after the Tao and follow what is natural. They abide by that which is empty and use stillness and clarity as their guide. They see life and death as parts of the same cycle and know that the ten thousand myriad things come from the same origin. They do not waste their energy because they know the importance of preserving the spirit. They hold on to simplicity and sleep without dreams. Their knowledge is hidden, and their actions are formless. They do not favor existence or nonexistence, life or death. Unhindered by form, they can move freely through different realms like deities and immortals.

Sages strengthen the spirit but do not let it dominate. Because they always dwell in the season of spring, for them there is no difference between day and night. They are at one with the cycle of growth, although their bodies do not feel it and their spirits do not experience it. They use the permanent to tame the impermanent, and their world has no beginning, no end, and no limit. They understand that all changes ultimately return to the formless source. Knowing that what is born does not experience birth and that what changes does not experience change, they live in the simplicity, humility, clarity, and primal oneness of the Tao.

## PART FOUR

# The Taoist in Spirit Life

*The Art of Being: Free and Easy Wandering*

Teachings from the *Zhuangzi*

# 12

# The Inner Chapters

## FREE AND EASY WANDERING

Peng Zu is said to have lived for eight hundred years; he is considered the longest-living person in humanity. He rode with the wind, floated among the clouds, and could travel ninety thousand miles in a day. Many marveled at his longevity and his abilities and would have given anything to be like him. However, if you think about it, eight hundred years is nothing compared to the timelessness of the Tao, the natural way. And ninety thousand miles is nothing measured against the limitlessness of the primordial. Small minds simply cannot know the vastness of consciousness.

The little cicada that can only flutter around the leaves of low branches and the dove that can only fly to the top of a tree cannot hope to have the vision of the eagle that glides and soars in the great expanse of the sky. The small mind is like the cicada and the dove: they are all limited by small understanding. And small understanding cannot lead to great understanding. Those who are short-lived cannot understand longevity, and those who are long-lived cannot understand timelessness. Mushrooms that sprout in the morning and die at noon do not know twilight, and insects that live only in summer can never experience autumn and winter. Only when you can merge with the limitless will you understand what it means to have no boundaries. Only when you can renew yourself with the cycles of the seasons will you understand what it means not to be bound by time.

It was said that Liezi could ride the wind and float with the clouds. Many would consider these to be incredible feats. But after soaring through the air for fifteen days, he had to return to earth. Even though Liezi could travel with the wind and the clouds, he was still dependent on them to carry him. Thus, his experience of wandering freely and easily in the void was at best sketchy.

There was once a sage named Song whose wisdom could earn him the highest office in the state. His honor was sufficient to command the respect of a community, his virtue was enough to impress a sovereign, and his talent was spectacular enough to land him any appointment in the country. However, Song had the same amount of pride as a little quail that knows it can fly only short distances. If the world sang his praises, Song did not exert more effort; if the world blamed him, he did not feel dejected. Not caged within the boundaries of fame and disgrace, he never fretted when faced with obstacles. Nor did he gloat with pride when he met with success. Not constrained by notions of accomplishment and failure, he had no sense of self, merit, or fame.

There was another man who lived on a mountain far to the west. His skin was soft like unblemished snow, and his demeanor was as gentle and unassuming as a young woman's. He did not eat grains but instead inhaled the wind and drank the dew. He would float up to the mist and clouds and wander through space beyond the four corners of the earth. Gathering and focusing the power of his spirit, he protected creatures from illness and made harvests bountiful. Even if flood waters were to rise up to the sky, he would not drown. Even if heat were to melt metal and scorch the earth, he would not be burned. This is because his virtue embraced the ten thousand things, and he was at one with all of them.

Of these four, Peng Zu and Liezi were still bound by time and space. Peng Zu's long years are nothing compared to timelessness, and Liezi's riding on the wind and clouds is nothing compared to simply merging with space. Only Song and the mountain hermit transcended the limits of space and time, for they rode on the truth of heaven and earth and floated with the changes of the seasons. This is truly free and easy wandering.

## ON ALL THINGS BEING EQUAL

Great understanding is broad; lesser understanding is picky. Great words carry strength; little words are petty and quarrelsome. When people go to sleep, their spirits get no rest. This is because during the day they are tangled up with everything they contact. Every day they use their minds to scheme. Some brag about themselves, some set traps for others, and some hide malicious intentions. Their small fears make them edgy and suspicious. Their big fears make them lose their minds. Some shoot off arguments like arrows and delight in bickering over right and wrong. Others hold on tightly to their opinions, certain they are correct. Squandering their life energy day after day, they are destined to fade and die like autumn leaves. Stuck in petty views and shallow concerns, they have abandoned that which is natural and limitless. Old and withering, their minds are near death, and nothing can restore them to life.

Rapture, anger, sadness, excitement, worry, regret, rashness, stubbornness, fear, carelessness, bluntness, and pretense are noises from empty hollows, bursting out like mushrooms from the damp ground. Day and night they spring up in front of us, and we don't even know where they come from.

Once we are born into the world, we hold on to life, anxious that it will end. Sometimes pushing ourselves forward, other times bowing down to hardship, we run our course in life like a wild horse galloping toward a cliff. Aren't we pathetic? Taxing our bodies and weakening our minds, we exhaust ourselves, not even knowing what we labor for. The body decays, and the mental clarity disappears—there's no greater sorrow than this.

Where there is birth, there will be death. Where there is death, there will be birth. Where there is acceptability, there will be unacceptability. Where there is recognition of what is right, there will be recognition of what is wrong. This is just the natural way of things. The sage rejects extremes and abides in the Way (the Tao), where no opposites exist. Petty people, however, wear out their brains trying to force equality on things. The sad part is that they don't know that things are naturally equal without us forcing equality on them. The Way can be said to be the Great Equalizer, for all things emerge from the same source, and being rooted in the Source, how could they not be equal?

Those who are learned believe that things do not exist and that nothing can be added to or subtracted from nonexistence. Those who are intelligent think that things exist but have no boundaries. Those who are wise recognize boundaries but see no right and wrong. When right and wrong appeared, the Way became obstructed, and because the Way is obstructed, we have notions of completeness and incompleteness, love and hate, gain and loss. The Way has never known boundaries. It's only because we started to favor "this" over "that" that boundaries started to appear. Boundaries are formed by distinctions, theories, concepts, discriminations, and assumptions. When boundaries emerge, there will be contention, disagreements, arguments, and bickering.

The Great Way cannot be named. Great clarity is never spoken, great virtue is not forced, great humility is not modest, and great courage does not attack. If the Way is conceptualized, it is not the Way. If clarity is put into discourse, it is no longer clear. If virtue has a standard, it cannot be universal. If humility is constrained by guidelines, it is no longer sincere. If courage is used to attack, it is no longer bravery. Therefore, to understand that some things cannot be fathomed is the greatest understanding. One who understands the Great Way—great clarity, great virtue, great humility, and great courage—is called the Reservoir of Heaven. Pour wisdom into this reservoir, and it is never filled. Take wisdom from it, and it will not run dry. Yet this reservoir does not know where its source comes from. This oblivion is called *hidden luminosity*.

The sage is merged with all things. This is why, when immersed in a blazing swamp, he is not burned, and when thrown into a freezing river, he is not chilled. Faced with lightning that splits the mountains and storms that toss the seas, he is not afraid. He rides the clouds and mist, walks with the sun and the moon, and wanders beyond the four corners of the earth.

If even death and life have no effect on the sage, how can she be affected by gain and loss? The sage embraces the sun, the moon, and the stars; holds the universe under her arm; merges with all things; and leaves confusion behind. The petty person is afraid that the world will end if she does not impress others, but the sage sits around like a block and attains simplicity in oneness.

Once Zhuangzi dreamed that he was butterfly, fluttering around aimlessly, happy, and carefree, not knowing that he was Zhuangzi the man. When he woke up, he was Zhuangzi the man again. Was he Zhuangzi the man dreaming that he was a butterfly, or was he a butterfly dreaming that he was Zhuangzi the man? Was there a transformation between the two, or were they one and the same?

Forget the boundaries, forget the distinctions. Plunge into the limitless and make it your home!

## NOURISHING LIFE

Those who know the importance of nourishing life will not expend their energy going after material things. Those who don't care about life will try to get what they desire at all cost. Those who understand the meaning of nourishing life know that conceptual thinking not only has limits but also wastes mental energy. If you use that which has limits to understand that which has no limit, you will attend to petty things and forget the big picture. Trying to grasp wisdom with concepts is no different from walking into a fire pit in front of you. Do good deeds, stay away from fame, follow the principle of moderation, and you will keep your sanity. Don't indulge in extremes, live simply, don't try to force things to go your way, and you will be around for a long time.

A good cook changes knives once a year; a mediocre cook changes knives once a month. This is because expert chefs care for their knives, whereas incompetent ones hack carelessly at meat and bones. Nourishing life is like caring for a knife. If you take care of your body and do not squander your energy, you will live for a long time.

When Laozi passed away, his friends went to his funeral to mourn him. Arriving at the burial site, they were surprised to find a large crowd of mourners: female and male, old and young. Laozi's passing was mourned by so many not because he was famous or learned but because he hid from the glamour, turned his back on the mundane, and never forgot what he was born with. He came when it was his time to come and departed when it was the natural thing to do. If you are content to follow the natural ways, then grief and happiness or fear and hope will not find a way to enter. This is called being freed from the bonds of limits and boundaries, and being free from limits and boundaries is what is meant by nourishing life.

## BEING IN THE WORLD

You need to know what you can do before you can help others. If you aren't sure of what you can do, it is no use trying to change the world.

Know what destroys virtue and know what knowledge can degenerate into. Virtue is destroyed by fame, and knowledge can degenerate into a tool for haggling. Fame can be used to coerce, and expertise can be used to barter. Knowledge, fame, and expertise can become weapons of destruction if used in the wrong way. If you are virtuous but don't understand people's minds, if you command respect but don't understand people's hearts, you are no different from a tyrant. Tyrants force their values on others. If you force your virtues, beliefs, and standards on others, everyone will see you as a plague.

It is best to hide wisdom within and allow those who want to display their cunning to argue over fine points. If you get yourself worked up over winning and losing, you'll soon find your eyes growing dim and your complexion becoming dull. Pretty soon, all you'll be able to think of is how to best others, and everything you say will become mindless excuses. You'll either become complacent or jump at every chance to please. You'll either give in to the whim of the crowd just to get support or be constantly afraid that your self-image will become tarnished. Once you are mired in this mess, you'll just sink deeper and deeper into suffering the rest of your life.

You might say, "What if instead of appearing righteous and benevolent, I am serious, diligent, and humble?" This is even worse. You can put on an impressive show of humility and dedication, but people are bound to see through your guise. They smell pretense and will never trust anything you say or do.

Or suppose you say, "I am inwardly true to myself but outwardly compliant and yielding. Being true to myself, I do not stray from virtue; being outwardly yielding, I can accommodate everything and be a companion to the world. Surely this is the best way to live in the world." This is just as bad. If your advice is not heeded, what will you do? Will you back off? You won't be blamed, but you won't be taken seriously, either. The moment you encounter obstacles, you deny they exist, using accommodation as an excuse.

Then what should you do? Don't listen with the ears; listen with your mind. Better yet, listen with your spirit instead of your mind. Your ears hear sounds but do not listen. Your mind recognizes things conceptually, but that's as far as it can go. Spirit, however, has no boundaries because it embraces all things. The Way gathers in stillness. When the mind does not feed itself with concepts, it abides in stillness, and spirit can take the honored place.

When you enter the service of a sovereign, go and play in the court but never be moved by fame. If your ruler listens, then sing. If he or she does not, then be silent. Don't open any gates. Better, don't even have a gate. Make oneness your home and accept that there will always be some things that cannot be avoided. Then you'll live in the world for a long time.

You can cheat people, but you can't cheat the Way. No doubt you've heard that realized beings can fly with wings and ride on the wind and the clouds. But do you know that it's possible to fly without wings or float without the support of clouds? You've heard of knowledge that knows, but have you heard of knowledge that does not know? Look inside the chamber where luminosity is born. Blessings gather when there is stillness that is both external and internal. If you sit like an unmoving log but your thoughts are racing, this is not stillness. Leave knowledge and concepts outside. Orient your awareness within, listen inwardly, and communicate with that which is inborn in you. This was how the sages changed the world.

In the world there are two movers of things: fate and duty. The bond between children and parents is one of fate. If you're bound by fate, there's little you can choose. Even if you hate your parents, they're still your parents. You can't undo this relationship. The bond between a subject and a ruler is one of duty. In duty there is honor and loyalty. If you serve a sovereign, you do so out of loyalty and love, knowing that there is no other place you want to be and no other thing you want to do. To honor your parents and to follow them anywhere is the pinnacle of filial gratitude. To serve your leader and do anything for him or her is the peak of loyalty. To serve your spirit so that it will not be injured by sadness, elation, fear, and arrogance is the epitome of nourishing life. To understand what can be done and what should be left alone is the perfection of virtue.

To speak of things that please two parties or anger both parties is very difficult. To please both parties, you must exaggerate positive points. To anger both parties, you must inflate the negatives. In both cases, you have to twist the truth, and this is utterly irresponsible. More-over, people will recognize exaggerations immediately, and consequently you'll never earn their trust. If you can't earn their trust, you'll be in danger. Therefore, stick to established facts and stay away from exaggeration.

When people play games, they often start out friendly. When the game turns into competition, people start getting angry and aggressive. If the competition continues, people resort to mean tricks. Action and speech become abusive, and friends end up punching each other.

When people meet at a celebration, they start out having drinks and joking with one another. If the party continues, the drinking gets heavier, the jokes become insults, and etiquette gives way to indulgence in unsavory amusements. It's the same with politics. You start out as a sincere and dedicated public servant, but once you're in office for a while, deceit and underhandedness creep in, and sincerity is forgotten. As in all things, what started out as simple ends up monstrous at the end because we are unable to let go when it's time to leave.

Words and actions are like wind and waves. They can stir up a storm at a moment's notice. Actions are swayed by gain and loss. They can enhance perceptions of gain and loss and lead to rash decisions. Anger is especially dangerous because it can muddle clear words and turn them into one-sided arguments.

Do not deviate from the natural ways, and do not push for perfection. To go beyond your limit is excessive. To try for completion is dangerous. What is not complete now may be complete later, and what is seemingly complete now may be incomplete when things run their course. It's best to just let things go their way. Be concerned only with things that can nourish you and stay away from things that lead you to harm. This was how the sages lived in the world.

How can you be an honest minister if you serve a nonvirtuous ruler? You can't let him do what he wants because his actions will ruin the nation. You can't teach him because you might get executed. What is the best course of action? First, be on your guard. Second, follow the ruler in his actions and make sure your thoughts are in harmony with his. However, while you follow his actions, do not get sucked in by them. Although you are in harmony with his thoughts, don't get drawn in by them. If you are pulled into your leader's unethical actions, you'll be overthrown and destroyed. If you get drawn in too far by his devious thoughts, you'll be blamed and condemned. Once you have mirrored him in thought and action, you will understand him thoroughly. When he sees that you understand him, you will gain his trust. When you have his trust, you can lead him onto the path of virtue.

When the world follows the way of virtue, the sage is not needed. When the world does not follow the way of virtue, the sage hides and survives. Cinnamon is a desired spice, so its tree is cut down; lacquer has a variety of uses, so its tree is mutilated. Everyone knows how the useful can be used, but no one knows the use of the useless.

## THE MARK OF VIRTUE

For those who embody virtue, life and death are important but have no hold on them. Even if the sky falls or the earth folds up, they feel no loss. Being able to see through the illusion of the transient nature of things, they are not flustered when things change. Yet even though they are at home with change, they also understand the constancy of the Way.

It would be silly to try to see a reflection of yourself in turbulent water. Only still waters can give you an accurate reflection of your face. In the same manner, only stillness can reflect stillness itself. In the natural world, only evergreen trees remain the same in both summer and winter. Of all those who receive life from the Source, only the sages stay above the ten thousand things. Because they live their lives according to the Way, they are able to care for the lives of others. The proof that someone is at one with the Way is their fearlessness. This person is not afraid to govern heaven and earth, although she understands that the body is just a temporary vessel. She is never separated from what she knows; therefore, her thoughts are limitless and her experiences are never stagnant.

Many people make excuses for their faults and shortcomings, claiming that they do not deserve to be punished. Few people, however, are able to admit their faults and, when spared, can say that they did not deserve to be let off the hook. To know that there are some things that you simply can't deal with and be content to accept it is the mark of one who embodies virtue.

Life, death, continuity, loss, failure, success, poverty, wealth, worthiness, unworthiness, slander, renown, hunger, thirst, cold, and heat are all part of the changing nature of things or, as some would say, destiny and fate. If you are in harmony with them, you will never be their servant. If you can hold this harmony day and night and blend with the change of the seasons, creating every moment and merging with it, this is virtue, and with it comes power.

Water is the most peaceful of things. Leave it alone, and it will be at rest. Therefore, water can serve as a standard for all of us. It sustains all yet shows no movement. Virtue is like water, sustaining all and being in harmony with all.

Knowledge is only one branch of a large tree. Promises are no better than adhesive tape and glue. Favors are useful only if a situation needs patching up, and skill is required only when you need to peddle your expertise. The sage therefore has no use for knowledge, promises, favors, and skill. He does not need to scheme and plot, so why does he need a lot of knowledge? She does not need to display glamour and glitz, so why does she need to patch up and cement relationships? He is not attached to gain and loss, so why does he need to curry and give favors? She has no expertise to sell, so why does she need to market her skill? Because he has no notions of this and that, the "should" and "should not," the correctness and incorrectness, cannot get him agitated. Massive, strong, and rooted, she rests alone in the perfection of the Way.

Those holding virtue do not allow likes and dislikes to disturb their stillness. They let things follow their natural tendencies and do not try to push them along. The Way gave them a face; heaven lent them a body. They are content with that. Many people, however, treat the spirit like an alien. They wear out their bodies, tire their minds, and dissipate their life force. Day after day, they lean against trees bemoaning their fate, slump at their desks and doze off, or lie on their beds dreading their burdens. The Way gave us each a healthy body and a sound mind. What a waste if we spend our lives sitting around like forgotten trash and jabber nonsense!

## THE GREAT TEACHER

Those who know the will of heaven and understand the actions of humanity are said to have attained ultimate knowledge. If you know the will of heaven, you'll be able to merge with heaven. If you understand the actions of humanity, you'll be able to use what you know to supplement what you don't know. Having these attainments should be sufficient to let you live out your life endowed by heaven. Most people will regard this achievement as the pinnacle of knowledge. But knowledge has limits: it must wait for the appropriate conditions before it can be applied. And anything that has to wait for the right circumstances to be effective is never certain. How do you know the will of heaven is truly the will of heaven and not the desires of humanity? Or vice versa? Only those with wisdom can see the difference.

Sages are sometimes called "great teachers." This is because they do not denigrate their needs, they are not proud of their fortune, and they do not scheme and plan for success. They may make mistakes but are not burdened by guilt. They can be successful, but they feel no need to brag about it. Never separated from the Way, they can climb peaks without fearing the height, enter water without getting wet, and walk through fire without being burned. They sleep without dreams and wake without being burdened by cares. They eat without craving, their breath originates deep within the belly, and they speak without pretense. In comparison, petty people breathe from the throat, their desires are deep, and their understanding of heaven is shallow. As a result, their words come out garbled, their speech is forced, and they spit out diatribes as if they are throwing up.

Sages do not understand what it means to love life and hate death. They come into the world without fanfare and leave without fussing. They come briskly without baggage and leave briskly without being encumbered. Although they do not forget where they came from, they do not think much of finding out where they will go after life. They received something good when they came into the world, and they delight in it. Upon leaving, they will hand it back without a second thought.

Life and death are part of the natural way of things, just as dawn and darkness are the natural ways of heaven. There are things that we can do and things that we can't do. The Way, Mother of all, gave you a body, filled it with life force, eases you into old age, and gives you rest in death. What else can you ask for? Think well of your birth, your health, your aging, and your death. Birth and death, youth and old age, beginning and end—delight in all of them.

The sage is not concerned with what is and what is not. Her face is serene and her forehead is wide. She can be chilly like an autumn wind and soft and warm like a spring breeze. Her joy and anger are natural, like the cycle of the seasons. In harmony with everything around her, she lets things follow their natural course and does not interfere with inborn nature. If she calls out the army to overthrow a nation, she will still have the hearts of the people. Such is the way of the sage.

Sages dwell in vastness. Their bearing is dignified; their view is lofty. They may not have everything in the world, but they are not tempted by gain and favors. They are sincere in their integrity but are never insistent; they are vast in their outlook but are never arrogant. Mild-mannered and always cheerful, they seem to be happy and carefree. Though unwilling to display expertise, they always help others by doing what is appropriate and necessary. Regardless of whether their actions are approved or disapproved, they do not hide behind a mask. Always relaxed, they rest in virtue. Tolerant and unassuming, they fit easily into the world. Above and alone, they are restricted by nothing. They know when to withdraw and when to engage.

For them, punishment and reward are like clothing worn on appropriate occasions. Rites and rituals are simply wings that take them to the vastness of the sky. Their wisdom comes from timeliness, their virtues from what is reasonable. Because they wear reward and punishment as garments, they can shed them easily and be compassionate and forgiving. Because they fly on the wings of rites and rituals into vastness, they can get along with the world perfectly. Because they see wisdom as that which is appropriate, they never stop doing what is meant to be done. Because they see virtue as something reasonable, they are able to plant their feet firmly on the ground while walking leisurely up the hill.

Yet for all this, people see them as just like any other individuals, having to work hard to get to where they are. Unbiased and free from likes and dislikes, they are simultaneously a companion of heaven and a friend of humanity. When humanity and heaven do not fight each other, sages become a natural part of society.

The Way is its own underlying reality. It is its own source and root. If it were handed to you, you couldn't receive it. If you tried to possess it, you would never get it. Before the cosmos was separated into heaven and earth, it was there. It gave luminosity to the spirits and deities; it gave birth to heaven and earth. Extending beyond the highest point, it cannot be labeled as lofty; reaching down to the uttermost depths, it cannot be regarded as deep. Because it already existed before heaven and earth arrived, its age cannot be determined. It was there before the beginning of time, yet you cannot say it is ancient.

Sages have no problem understanding the Way. Counting to three, they can put the world outside themselves. Counting to seven, they can put everything inside themselves. Counting to nine, they can attain the brightness of dawn. And in experiencing the dawn, they see their own aloneness. When they realize they are utterly alone, they can lay aside past and present. When they can dispense with past and present, they are able to transcend life and death. For the sage, there is nothing to send away, nothing to welcome, nothing to destroy, and nothing to complete.

Fish cannot survive without water, and humanity cannot survive without being part of the Way. If you dig a pond and fill it water, fish will swim in it contentedly. If you let humanity follow the natural ways, people's lives will be peaceful and secure. When fish are in their natural environment, water, they forget they are surrounded by water. When humans are in their natural environment, the Way, it does not occur to them that they are surrounded by the Way. Go with the natural way of things. Don't bother to force things along. With this, you'll merge with the profound oneness of all.

## WORTHY OF BEING A SOVEREIGN

When a sage governs, he does not follow guidelines and principles like an amateur cook following a recipe from a cookbook. He looks within, makes sure that what he is going to do is appropriate, and determines that his thoughts and actions are not against virtue. The sage wanders in simplicity, blends with vastness, and follows the natural way of things. There is simply no room for personal views and petty concerns. It is in this way that the sage rules the world.

The achievements of an enlightened ruler pervade the kingdom, but they do not appear to be her doings. Her influence reaches everywhere, but her subjects are not dependent on her. There is no promotion and no praise; there is only enjoyment. The ground she stands on cannot be fathomed. Where she dwells, there is no place for gain and loss.

Do not go after fame and recognition. Don't scheme. Don't be obsessed with achievements. Don't get bogged down by projects for the sake of doing projects. Embody fully that which has no beginning and no end; wander where there are no trails. Hold on to what heaven and earth have endowed you with, but don't think you've gotten everything.

The sage uses his mind like a mirror: reflecting things as they are, judging nothing, retaining nothing, and adding nothing. In this way he wins without bringing harm to himself and others.

There is a story about Liezi before he understood what it means to be enlightened. Hearing that there was a shaman who could perform incredible feats, he went to see for himself what this man could do. Indeed, the shaman could walk through fire, hold his breath for hours, and predict and control the weather. Thoroughly impressed, Liezi went to his teacher Huzi, claiming that he had found the ultimate realized being. Huzi made no comment, asking only if he could meet the shaman himself.

Liezi brought the shaman to see Huzi. After taking a look at Huzi, the shaman ran out to find Liezi. "Your teacher is dying," he said. "When I saw him, he was like a sack of wet ashes, heavy, inert, and lifeless." Distressed, Liezi reported the shaman's observations to his teacher. Huzi laughed and said, "I am not dying. I just appeared to him as the primal earth, silent and unmoving like a big lump of sod."

The next day, the shaman went to see Huzi again. Beckoning to Liezi, who was waiting outside Huzi's home, the shaman said, "Today your teacher is better. He now has the breath of life and will regain his vitality soon. I believe my presence has cured him of the sickness he was afflicted with." When Liezi reported this to his teacher, Huzi said, "Today I chose to appear to him as heaven and earth copulating. What he saw was the workings of yin and yang rising from my heels to the top of the head. Get your shaman to visit me again."

The shaman paid Huzi a visit the next day. This time, he observed Huzi for a long time and then left quietly. When Liezi asked what condition his teacher was in, the shaman exclaimed, "Your teacher is shifting and changing all the time. I can't read his behavior, nor his facial features, nor his destiny. Even the positions of the stars change around him. I will see him again when he is more stable."

When Huzi received this report from Liezi, he said, "Today I became the great vastness of space where there is no this and that, where there is only the continuous rise and fall of the original breath. Where the waters swirled, he saw an abyss. Where the waters were silent, he saw an abyss. Where the waters were running, he also saw an abyss. Everything he saw was an abyss! Get him to come again."

Not believing what he had seen in his previous visits, the shaman called on Huzi again. This time, the moment the shaman stepped into the room where Huzi was sitting, he ran out in alarm. Liezi tried to stop the shaman to ask for an explanation, but the man had disappeared. Liezi returned to his teacher and asked, "What happened?" Huzi replied, "I finally showed him the state of 'not having emerged from the source yet.' I was empty of thought, feeling, perception, and bodily form. Floating, sinking, turning, wriggling, I displayed no notions of who, what, when, and how. He was so scared that he ran away!"

After this incident, Liezi began to understand the teachings of Huzi. He realized that he had been fascinated by the tricks of conjurers and the casual sorcery of magicians and that he had abandoned the way of simplicity and vastness. Liezi went home and meditated for three years. When he came out of his retreat, he was a simple man. Daily he farmed his fields. He cooked for his wife, cleaned the house, and fed the pigs as if they were his guests. He got rid of the ornate, the glamorous, and the polished. Returning to uncarved plainness and simplicity, he delighted in everything but was not attracted to anything. He felt everything but was not tethered to anything. He was immersed in the dust of the world, but these entanglements did not drain him. He lived out the rest of his life in oneness and simplicity.

# 13

# The Outer Chapters

## WEBBED TOES

A person with webbed toes is someone who has grown a useless part of the body. Only frogs and other creatures that spend most of their lives swimming in water need to have webbed toes. Not only is it unnecessary for people to have webbed toes, it is actually a liability. *Web-toed* is therefore a term we use to refer to something superfluous, needless, and inappropriate.

People who are said to be web-toed in their sight are dazzled by superfluous and useless designs. Those who are web-toed in hearing are enchanted by pleasing words and addicted to noise and senseless babble. Unable to appreciate silence, they feel uncomfortable once the auditory stimulation stops. Those who are web-toed in speech speak with forked tongues, mangling virtue and manipulating benevolence for personal gain. To acquire fame and fortune or to get vengeance, they will whip up a storm of spite in the name of service toward an ideal. They tear apart inborn nature, giving in to greed, revenge, and hate. Those who are web-toed in a discourse try to win debates by using cross-examination, twisted logic, and paradoxes. They thread their thoughts through useless words and fabricated differences, thus keeping themselves from the path of truth and virtue.

In contrast, those who embrace virtue are not web-toed in sight, hearing, speech, or action. Having never lost their connection to their inborn nature of goodness, they do not delight in the superfluous and the useless. They abide in the constancy of the natural world, and their measure of length is never too long or too short. In this natural constancy, things are not twisted by logic, straightened by force, rounded by molding, squared by cutting, joined by glue, or bound together by rope and twine. Grounded in their natural interdependency, things are round, square, straight, or curved because that's the way they are, not because they were forced to be so.

In a world immersed in virtue, people live in contentment, not knowing what makes them content. Their lives are simple, uncomplaining, and unadorned. They don't need wits and guile to get around in the world because there is no place for scheming. They understand that expertise has nothing to do with benevolence and virtue. You can be an expert in a skill, like carpentry, but you cannot be an expert in virtue. To claim to be expert in virtue means that you are manipulating virtue to your use. Virtue that is manipulated is no longer virtue. Benevolence that is applied is no longer benevolence. True virtue and benevolence are inborn and cannot be improved upon or applied.

People who look at others and not at themselves will see only what others have. As a result, they will seek to gratify themselves with what others have but never see what they have. They will try to emulate the thoughts and actions of others but never delight in their inborn nature. They will try to figure out what brings joy to others but will never know how to bring joy into their own lives.

## HORSES AND PEOPLE

Horses are meant to run free; their hooves are made to endure frost, snow, grass, and sand. They shed their coats in summer to keep cool and build a thick coat in winter to keep warm. Although they may be kept inside palaces and fine stables, they really have no need for these types of lodging.

Then along come the horse trainers, who claim to breed horses for specific needs. So now we have racehorses, show horses, war horses, and carriage horses. If there were no desire for the pleasure of racing, there would be no racehorses. If there were no amusement in watching horses perform, there would be no show horses. If there were no need for war, there would be no war horses. If people lived simple lives, preferring to walk rather than be carried around in vehicles, there would be no need for carriage horses.

In order to improve breeding and train horses for special uses, the horse trainers geld those of lesser breeding, starve and strangle them into submission, force them to run side by side and respond to bit and rein, and make them cower in terror of whip and bridle. By the time the horse trainers have obtained what they want, half the horses have not survived. If there were no demand for special horses, there would be no demand for trainers and breeders, and the horses would be left to their inborn nature.

Handling the affairs of the state is like handling horses. Only those who desire to dominate would rule by fear and terror, whipping and starving citizens into submission. Only those who seek to conquer the world would train soldiers by subjecting them to routines that maim and injure the recruits. Only those who desire to control every behavior of their subjects would force their people to think and act the way they dictate. Only those who do not command respect naturally would force submission with the threat of punishment.

The sagely ruler does nothing like this but instead lets the people follow their inborn nature: weaving threads for clothing, farming land for food, and celebrating as a community when the occasion calls for it. This is called sharing virtue. When virtue pervades society, people's gait is slow and relaxed, and their gaze is soft and steady. Roads are not cut through mountains, rivers are not dammed, and forests are not cleared. Birds can nest near villages without fear of being hunted, wild animals do not prey on domestic animals, and children do not need to run from strangers. Because people are simple and honest and do not know what it means to scheme, their thoughts and actions are not distorted by ambition and technical know-how. Free of desire, they abide in a simplicity that is uncarved and unadorned. In this way they are never separated from their inborn and true nature.

If virtue and the natural way of things were not abandoned, there would be no need for rules, regulations, or even the teaching of kindness and benevolence. If unborn nature were not ignored, there would be no need for rituals, rites, and ethics. If people were not trapped by sensual pleasures, there would be no place for fads and fashions.

People abandoned the Way because they thought they could improve on something that is actually best left alone. The natural ways were abandoned when the artisan decided that human activity could outdo natural beauty. They were abandoned when rulers believed that laws and justice could replace virtue.

When horses are left alone to roam the fields, they eat the grass and drink from the streams. In mating season, they procreate. In natural affection, they rub their necks against each other. In competing for a mate, they kick and scream. This is what horses naturally do. Force them to race or pull heavy loads, and they will rip the hitches, injure the handlers, or topple the carriage. If horses can resort to destructive behavior when forced to do what is not their inborn nature, imagine what people will do when they are forced to go against their inborn nature!

The sagely rulers ruled by not ruling. People stayed at home when they needed to be at home and traveled only when they needed to go somewhere. They farmed, wove, cooked, and traded as they felt the need. Their mouths were full, and they were happy. Patting their bellies, they passed their time in contentment. Then along came those who wanted to motivate people to do more, have more, and want more. People learned to covet knowledge and know-how; they fought over profit and loss; they schemed to be more prosperous, more famous, and more powerful than those around them. Once these changes occurred, it became difficult to return to the inborn nature of simplicity.

## RIFLING THROUGH BOXES

Someone who plans to guard against thieves who rifle through boxes will put locks on the containers. Believing that the goods are secure, the person will proceed to pile more treasures into the locked chests. Locks may deter the petty thief, but a smart thief will simply haul away the boxes and break the locks later.

If you don't put locks on boxes, then you are bound to put fewer possessions in them, and when you're robbed, you'll lose less. If you lock the boxes, however, you'll have a false sense of security. As a result, you will put more treasures in the boxes and end up losing more. So piling up possessions just means that you'll invite smarter thieves. Similarly, piling up laws and regulations means that you'll encourage more ingenious ways of breaking them. If you don't want thieves rifling through your boxes, then cultivate simplicity. With simplicity, what is stored will not be perceived as treasures. When there is no perceived value in the contents of the boxes, thieves will not be interested in stealing what's in there.

Just as fish should not be taken out of deep pools, weapons should not be shown publicly. Fish thrive in deep water, and sages thrive in anonymity. When sages seek publicity and try to distinguish themselves, they are no longer sages. They begin to see the practice of virtue as a profession rather than a state of being. In this way, they are no different from the criminal who sees crime as a normal career.

The sage is a like a sharp weapon. This weapon should never be displayed and should be used only out of necessity. It is better if the sage never gets to use his wisdom. It is said that when there is no desire for war, there will be no need for a military presence. Even peacekeeping forces will be out of work!

Set up a system of weights and measures, and people will figure out ways to cheat it. Promote ethics, and people will exhibit benevolent actions but have criminal thoughts. Put a value on gold, jade, and jewelry, and thieves will multiply. Reward ambitious behaviors and intentions, and people will resort to unscrupulous ways to obtain favors.

The world has gone awry because people in positions of leadership abandon their responsibilities once they have attained wealth and reputation. They pack up their belongings and dash off to exotic places. They abandon their families, serve causes that give them the most profit, and do not hesitate to betray their home country for favors abroad. This happens when people forsake the Way and follow personal ambition.

When ambition becomes the root of knowledge, knowledge and technology will develop to serve control and conquest. When knowledge is developed for making bows and arrows, birds will flee to the skies. When knowledge is used to make dragnets, fish will disappear into the ocean depths. When knowledge is used to make traps and snares, wild animals will hide in the forests and mountains. When knowledge is used to fashion weapons of destruction, sages will live in oblivion. When the Way is abandoned, confusion will reign.

Confusion is so destructive that it can block the brightness of the sun and the moon, scorch fields and hills, dry up rivers and lakes, and overturn the cycles of the seasons. It can push aside honest and simple people in favor of those who are ambitious and ruthless. It can draw people away from calm nonaction and drive them into a frenzy of jumbled and endless chattering.

If you can get people to turn their senses away from external things, they will be able to look inward. Looking inward, they will regain true sight. When people have true sight, the world will no longer look dazzling. If the world is no longer perceived as glamorous, people will no longer desire to be stimulated by sights and sounds every moment of their waking lives. Consequently, they can begin to cultivate a silent appreciation of their surroundings. When people hold on to their inborn wisdom, the world will no longer appear confused. When people do not lose their connection to virtue, the world will no longer feel crazy.

## LEAVE IT ALONE

Let the world be; leave it alone. Don't try to manipulate and control it. Otherwise, you will abandon the Way and distract people from virtue. If the natural order of things is not disrupted, if people don't stray from virtue, there will be no need for laws and administration.

If you are excessively happy, you will damage the yang within. If you are excessively angry, you will damage the yin within. When yin and yang are damaged, the seasons will become untimely and the world will become unsettling and confusing. Heat and cold will be out of harmony, people will be restless, and illness will increase. Unable to balance happiness and anger, people will move impatiently from place to place, think up schemes that lead to nothing, and argue with no conclusions.

Although everyone seems to agree that virtuous people should be rewarded, there appears to never be enough reward. Although everyone seems to agree that unethical people should be punished, there appears to never be enough punishment. Ever since there has been government and large bureaucracy, people have fussed over rewards and punishments, debating over how they should be given and in what amount. Constantly arguing for the sake of arguing, how can people ever have time to rest in the inborn nature of virtue?

Become attached to what you see, and you'll be blinded by shapes and colors. Become attached to what you hear, and you'll be deafened by the roar of sounds. Become attached to benevolence, and you'll bring confusion to virtue. Become attached to etiquette, and you'll be trapped in artificiality. Become attached to correctness, and you'll abandon compassion. Become attached to knowledge, and you'll encourage petty faultfinders. Become attached to being a sage, and you'll end up abandoning the Way. As long as you rest in the inborn nature, it does not matter whether there are sights, sounds, benevolence, rites, rituals, knowledge, and wisdom. If you do not rest in the inborn nature, these things will get warped and be blown out of proportion.

There's nothing wrong with delighting in sights, sounds, benevolence, etiquette, music, propriety, knowledge, and becoming a sage. It becomes a problem only when we become attached to them. Enjoy the delight by resting in these things rather than wanting to have them. Once you promote, reward, cherish, and value them, you'll be on the road to delusion.

It was said that after the Yellow Emperor ruled for nineteen years, his commands were followed and respected by all his subjects. Believing that he could still improve his leadership skills, he went to the sage Guangzhen for advice. The emperor bowed before the sage and said, "I would like to learn about the essence of heaven and earth so that I can apply it to help the grains to grow. I want to master yin and yang so that I can use it nourish the earth and my people. Can you teach me?"

Guangzhen replied, "It looks like you want to learn about the natural order of things in order to control them. When you control the natural order, the natural order is no longer natural. How can something that is not natural give birth to and nourish all things? You've turned government into control and benevolence into mere behavior. Ever since you ascended the throne, rain has fallen before the clouds gathered, leaves have fallen before they turned yellow, and the light of the sun and the moon have grown weaker every day. This is all because of your wanting to control everything. You stupid and arrogant man, how can you be taught the Way?"

The Yellow Emperor returned home and spent three months living in a straw hut in solitary retreat. Then he humbly went to Guangzhen again for advice. This time he crawled on his hands and knees to where the sage was meditating and said, "Please teach me how to live a long and healthy life."

Guangzhen opened his eyes, saw the Yellow Emperor's sincerity, and said, "You are now ready to learn. The Way is fathomless, hidden, dark, and silent. When there is no seeing and no hearing, the body will regulate itself. Be still in thoughts, do not tire your body with labor, do not churn up your desire, and you will live a long life. When the eye does not see, when the ears no longer hear, and when the mind no longer wants to know, the spirit will embrace and protect the body, and the body will enjoy health and longevity. Don't get carried away by what is inside. Block off what is intruding from the outside. Too much knowledge will harm the spirit. Too much physical labor will harm the body. Too much indulgence will harm the essence of life. Once you understand this, I will show you the path through the Great Luminosity to the source of pure yang and guide you through the dark Mysterious Gate to the source of pure yin. Heaven and earth have their masters, and yin and yang have their storehouses. Take care of your own body. Guard it from things that can harm it. Then the sky and earth, the yin and yang, within you will grow strong."

The Yellow Emperor prostrated, thanked Guangzhen, and asked, "What is the Source and the Great Harmony?"

Guangzhen replied, "They are inexhaustible, yet people think that they have a beginning and an end. They are unfathomable, yet people think they can be measured. Those who embody them within will be luminous. Above they will merge with vastness; below they will rule and protect the earth. Those who fail to embody them will remain trapped in the muck of confusion. Now that I have given you pointers to the Way, it's up to you to enter the gate of the inexhaustible, wander freely in the limitless, merge with the sun and the moon, and rest with the constancy of heaven and earth. What is before me, I embrace; what is beyond me, I let merge with darkness."

Rest in nonaction and stillness, and things will transform by themselves. Don't be preoccupied with form, do not be attached to the senses, and forget that you are a thing among other things; then you'll be able to join with the deep and fathomless. Untangle the mental knots, cast off thoughts, be blank and unresponsive, and you will return to the root of all things without knowing how and why. Tumbling within the dark and undifferentiated chaos, you'll never be separated from the Origin. But if you try to analyze it, you will already have separated yourself from it. Don't ask its name; don't try to figure out its form. Simply leave it alone and let it be.

The teachings of the sagely ruler is like a shadow. Although it follows principles, it has no form. Although it can be heard, it is like an echo that simply mirrors a sound. The sage answers only when there are questions. Then she pours out her thoughts and makes herself a friend to all. She lives in the void, moves without direction, and takes you by the hand to lead you to return to the Source. Wandering freely in that which has no beginning and no end, she weaves in and out of the limitless. Ageless as the sun, she blends with the Great Unity. Selfless, she is not bound to anything. Not being bound to anything, how can she have possessions? Being limitless, how can she be trapped by things meaningful and meaningless? Those who fix their attention on possessions were called sensible in ancient times. But those who turn their awareness on nothingness are the true friends of heaven and earth.

Even the lowliest things have their use. Even the most mundane people can be given responsibilities. Even the most annoying affairs must be attended to. Even though laws have loopholes, they must still be enforced. Even though integrity is necessary to form distant relationships, it must be practiced. Even though benevolence may affect only those near you, the extent of its influence cannot be doubted. Even though rituals can be tedious sometimes, they must be practiced repeatedly. Even though virtue cannot be separated from humanity, it must be embraced tirelessly. Even though the Way is part of the natural order, it still has to be adapted to circumstances. Even though the way of heaven is inherently spiritual, it still has to be put into action.

The sage contemplates heaven but does not help it along. He contemplates virtue but does not need to embellish it. He acts in accordance to the Way but does not plan to do it deliberately. He exercises benevolence but does not brag about it. He draws inspiration from integrity but does not need to force it to happen. He participates in rituals but does not shun or wallow in them. He does not make excuses when he needs to get rid of things.

The sage adopts laws and regulations to avoid confusion. She asks people to assist her without being totally dependent on them or dismissive of their contributions. She knows tools are useful under certain circumstances but does not discount them or become attached to them when the task is completed. She does not believe that things are either useful or useless because she knows that use and nonuse change according to circumstances.

Those who do not understand the Way will not be pure in virtue. Consequently they will not be able to find an appropriate path in life. This is pitiful indeed!

The Way is that which is natural; it is the path of the immortals.

There is also the mundane and petty way, which is *not* the Way. To rest in nonaction and command respect is the natural Way. To use force in action and become entrapped in it is the mundane and petty way. The path to immortality is about becoming simpler and simpler each day. The path of pettiness is about increasing complexity day after day.

## HEAVEN AND EARTH

Heaven and earth are both primal, but they manifest themselves differently. Although there are myriad things, they come from the same source. Although there are numerous citizens in a kingdom, they are all subjects of the same sovereign. The sovereign finds meaning in ruling by connecting to virtue and the Way. The sagely sovereigns of ancient times ruled through nonaction, doing nothing more than being grounded in virtue.

If the light of the Way illuminates the world, the sovereign will be virtuous. If the light of the Way illuminates the relationship of the ruler and the ruled, the duties of the sovereign and the ministers will be clear. If the light of the Way illuminates the abilities of the ministers, the affairs of the country will be organized. If the light of the Way illuminates everywhere, the creation and nourishment of the ten thousand things will be complete.

The Way pervades heaven and earth. Virtue flows through all the myriad things. When there is natural order between those who rule and those who serve, we call this good administration. When abilities are trained and used appropriately, we call this good skill. Good skill is a part of good administration. Good administration comes from dedication. Dedication is rooted in virtue. And virtue is tied to the Way. In ancient times the sagely rulers followed the way of virtue. When virtue was followed, the people were content and satisfied. When the people are content, the nation will be peaceful. When nations are peaceful, there will be no wars abroad and no violence at home.

Heaven is so vast that it encompasses the ten thousand things; earth is so great that it can support them. To follow the ways of heaven and earth is to act through nonaction. To embody virtue is to speak through nonaction. To care for all beings by bringing benefits to all is called benevolence. To be able to go beyond barriers and fixedness is called freedom. To possess the ten thousand things and not be possessed by them is called wealth. To embrace virtue and not budge from it is called being rooted in the Origin. To grow into virtue is called maturity. To follow the Way is called fruition. Not allowing external stimulation to disrupt your stillness is called perfection.

Hide your gold in the mountains. Bury your jewels in the ocean depths. When you see no gain in accumulating and displaying money and goods, when you are not excited by wealth and status, when you are not particularly happy about long life or sad about early death, when social recognition no longer attracts you, when you find no shame in poverty and no aversion toward wealth, you won't be interested in robbing others to build your hoard or flaunting your wealth to gain power and win admiration.

Those who possess virtue embrace simplicity and do not wish to be a master of facts and details. Standing on the ground of the Origin, their understanding reaches not only people but also ghosts and spirits. Because their virtue reaches far, their thoughts emerge only when necessary. Without the Origin, bodies cannot have life; without virtue, life cannot have clarity. To preserve the body and live a long and healthy life, to uphold virtue and make clear the Way—this is virtue. Vast, boundless, suddenly emerging, suddenly dissolving, moving this way and that, inspiring the ten thousand things without fanfare—such are those who embody virtue. Those who embody virtue can see in complete darkness and hear in complete silence. In the midst of darkness, they alone see the light of dawn; in the midst of silence, they alone hear harmony. Hiding in the shadowy depths, tangled among layers of spirituality, they alone discover the true inner essence.

In the primal beginning, there was the void. The void has no name or substance. Out of the void emerged the One that has no form. When the One awoke and came to life, it was called virtue. The One transformed and became two. From the flow and flux of the two, things came into being, each taking on its distinctive form, though still connected to the One. Within each form is inborn nature. Form has limitations and characteristics, but inborn nature does not. Inborn nature is inseparable from virtue, and virtue in its highest manifestation is identical to the primal beginning. Cultivate virtue, and you will be no different from the primal beginning. Being no different from the primal beginning, you will be empty; being empty, you will be clear; being clear, you will be pure; being pure, you will be great; being great, you will be able to merge with heaven and earth. This joining of heaven and earth is wild and spontaneous; it is free from the dualities of rudeness and courtesy, stupidity and ingenuity; and it will send you deep into the swirling chaos of primal virtue.

When a great sage rules, he creates conditions to allow people's minds to be vast, free, and far wandering. He simplifies custom, etiquette, and sophistication and allows people to act according to their inborn nature. Thus he removes meaning from treason and rebellion.

Those who embrace the Way are complete in virtue. If you are complete in virtue, you'll be complete in body. Being complete in body, you'll be complete in spirit. And being complete in spirit is the mark of the sage. When you are content to live in simplicity, then achievement, profit, fame, and fortune will have no place in your life. When praised, you won't be concerned; when blamed, you'll be serene and calm. Letting body and spirit follow the inborn nature, you can wander freely through the everyday world and not be flustered. Completely hidden in the midst of society, your external appearance will be like any other person's, but internally you will be merged with the primal simplicity and returned to true luminosity and purity.

When a sage governs, she assigns duties so that the abilities of the ministers fit the tasks. She promotes them so that no talent goes to waste. She knows the skills of her subjects and puts them where they are best for the country. She has no time for flatterers or the incompetent. It is not that she is not compassionate; it is because she knows that incompetence will harm the people, and flattery will get nothing done. The government of the sage has no need for edicts, commands, threats, or enticements. With only a simple nod or a wave of her hand, people will come flocking to assist her.

Those who embody virtue have no bias toward beauty and against ugliness. They see situations beyond right and wrong. They share happiness with those who are joyful, sadness with those who suffer, bewilderment with those who have lost their way, and amusement with those who are fascinated with a new discovery. Such is the person who has embraced virtue.

Those who cultivate the essence of life are able to eject the spirit to ride the light when the body dissolves. The light is the radiance that illuminates vastness. These people live out their lives following their inborn nature. In life they rest in the joyful flux of heaven and earth. In death they merge with the dark and undifferentiated chaos and return to the oblivion from which they originally came.

When virtue rules, the virtuous are not employed and the talented are not sought after. Everyone does what is appropriate without knowing the principles of right and wrong. They care for one another but have no idea that this is called benevolence. They are true to the inborn nature but have no concept of loyalty. They are trustworthy but do not know the meaning of honesty. They perform all kinds of services for one another but do not know that this is being kind. In this way, they move through their lives without leaving tracks and footprints. Acting naturally, they arrive without fanfare and depart without leaving a trace.

When virtue is abandoned, people agree with what is popular and do things to please the crowd. Public opinion, not inborn nature, and not even the conviction of right and wrong, dictates beliefs and actions. Leaders polish arguments and speak pleasing words to gain support. Followers are enticed by petty promises and gains. Those in government display their skills in the hope of attaining wealth and advancement. Abandoning the principles of right and wrong, they brag about their leadership skills while belittling others. Yet all this time they have failed to see themselves as one of the mob.

Those who know that they are fools are not the biggest fools. Those who know that they are confused are not as confused as they think they are. The most confused are those who live their entire lives not knowing the straight from the crooked. The biggest fools are those who in all their lives have never seen the light of virtue and have never even aspired to see that light.

When colors and shapes confuse the eyes, the eyesight will be unclear. When noise and dissonance confuse the ears, the hearing will be dulled. When odors overstimulate the nose, headaches will occur. When flavors inundate the mouth, the sense of taste will be impaired. When likes and dislikes dominate thoughts, people will be volatile and unable to hold on to their inborn nature. Thus, overloading your senses and crowding your mind with too many opinions can be a dangerous thing.

## THE WAYS OF HEAVEN

It is natural for heaven to keep moving and not be fixed. In this way the myriad things can come to fruition. It is natural for a ruler to keep moving and not be fixed. In this way, the world can be made whole. It is natural for the sage to keep moving and not be fixed. In this way humanity can aspire to be like him. To understand the ways of heaven, to be a friend of wisdom, to walk the path of virtue, and to dwell in stillness dreamily all come naturally to the sage. The sage does not abide in stillness because she believes that stillness is good and desirable. Rather, it is because it is the natural thing to do. Just as a pool of still water gives a clear image of everything reflected in it, the stillness that the sage abides in is the perfect mirror of heaven and earth and the ten thousand things.

Emptiness, simplicity, silence, and stillness are the natural tendencies of heaven and earth. Rest in emptiness, and you will be full and complete. Rest in stillness, and you will accomplish without action. Rest in simplicity, and you will be joyful, and when you take joy in simplicity, you will be free from anxiety over gain and loss. Rest in silence, and you will preserve the spirit and live a long and healthy life.

Emptiness, simplicity, silence, and stillness form the root of the ten thousand things. To be able to embody them is the mark of an enlightened ruler. To be able to apply them is the mark of an enlightened minister. To be able to hide them is the mark of the dark sage, the shadow adviser. To rest in them is to lead a life of free and aimless wandering. To embrace them is to be at one with the rivers and the seas, the hills and the forests. To emerge with them is to engage the world. To act in them is to rule a harmonious and peaceful society. Rest in stillness, and you will be a sage. Rest in action, and you will be a ruler. Rest in silence, and you will be honored. Rest in simplicity, and no one will compete with you.

Those who have a clear view of virtue and the ways of heaven and earth are called the Great Ancestors. They are in harmony with the ways of heaven, and being in harmony with heaven, they bring harmony to humanity. To harmonize with fellow beings is called human joy; to harmonize with the ways of heaven is called celestial joy. In passing judgment, the sage does not consider himself severe. In extending his bounty to all, he does not consider himself altruistic. Older than the oldest, he does not think he is long-lived. Above he covers heaven, and below he supports the earth. He creates and destroys the ten thousand forms but does not consider himself skilled. Dwelling in the joy of heaven, he knows that life is simply the workings of heaven and that death is part of the natural transformation of things. In stillness, he partakes in the yin. In motion, he flows with the yang. Those who dwell in the joy of heaven incur no wrath from heaven, no opposition from humanity, no entanglement from things, and no harm from ghosts and spirits. In movement they embody the ways of heaven; in stillness they embrace the ways of earth.

The sage experiences heavenly joy whether she leads the world in motion or rests in stillness. The virtues of a sagely ruler are rooted in heaven and earth. Since heaven and earth naturally tend to be still, the sagely ruler, abiding in this stillness, can lead the world with time to spare. The superior ruler applies nonaction, and the world follows her naturally. The inferior ruler forces things along, and the world drags after her unnaturally. The enlightened ruler possesses knowledge and wisdom as great as heaven and earth, but that wisdom is never forced. Although her understanding surpasses that of the greatest thinkers, she does not expound theories. Although her abilities outshine all, she does not attempt to make things happen. Knowing that heaven gives birth and that earth bestows nourishment without making an effort, she rests with the Source and lets her subordinates deal with the trivial. The essence of ruling lies in the ruler; the details of running a kingdom lie with the ministers.

The ruler rules according to the principles of virtue. The ministers work in the details of virtue. Giving rewards and punishments and calculating benefits and penalties are the details of public administration. Rituals and laws, weights and measures, and management of public servants are the details of efficient government. Setting standards for fabricating musical instruments and training musicians are the details of making music. Setting guidelines for mourning, funeral rites, and burials are the details of the protocol of grieving. However, while ministers need to be diligent in attending to the details of virtue, they must also be inspired by the movement of the spirit in the leader. Without spirit, details become mindless trivia and forms become empty functions.

The ruler leads; the ministers follow. The parents provide; the children benefit. The sage teaches; the people are inspired. What is above is honored, and what is below is commanded. These are the workings of heaven and the natural way of things. Heaven is above; earth is below. Spring precedes summer, summer is followed by autumn, and autumn is followed by winter. This is the natural sequence of the seasons. The transformations of birth, growth, death, and decay are part of the natural order of things.

The sagely ruler understands the Way and is intimate with the workings of heaven. Being intimate with the ways of heaven, he embodies virtue naturally. Embodying virtue, he can apply its details. Having clarity in the details of virtue, he can do his duties without bias. Knowing how to apply virtue, he is able to assign responsibilities according to the abilities of his subordinates. Having assigned responsibilities, he can observe the performance of his subordinates and give rewards and punishments.

In this way, good and competent people will be used to the best of their abilities. Those with a deep understanding of virtue are put in leadership positions; those with a lesser understanding of virtue are placed in adjutant positions. Without scheming and plotting, everyone and everything will find its right place under heaven. This is called the Great Peace, the highest form of governance.

To give rewards and punishments without understanding the ways of heaven is like counting coins without understanding the value of money. To give a discourse on forms without understanding the ways of heaven is to be disconnected from the Source. To impose law and order without understanding the ways of heaven can only bring about a temporary and uneasy peace. To be familiar with the methods of bringing order but not understand the ways of heaven allows you to work for the world but does not get the world to work for you.

Heaven and earth follow a constant. The sun and the moon have their natural brightness. Stars and planets have their locations in the sky. Birds and beasts relate to their own kind. Trees and grass grow only where the climate is appropriate for them. If you go along with virtue, you will naturally walk the path of the Way.

The Way is not intimidated by the high and mighty. It is not demeaning toward the low and tiny. Myriad things are created and nourished by it. Vast, subtle, and simple, it receives and accommodates everything. Deep and profound, it cannot be fathomed. Rules, regulations, rites, rituals, rewards, and punishments are all subsumed under the Way. Although they are trivial to the spirit, the enlightened ruler knows their value and puts them in the rightful place in governance. The sagely ruler cranks the handle that turns the world but does not manage the workings. She sees through falsehood but is not distracted by thoughts of gain and loss. She identifies truth in the midst of confusion but does not cling to it. Putting aside life and death, even heaven and earth, she is not preoccupied with the myriad things. Being free from the ten thousand concerns, her spirit will never be weakened.

## THE TURNING OF THE HEAVENS

Do the heavens turn? Do the stars march through the sky? Is the earth still? Do the sun and the moon compete in their brightness? Who is in charge of all this? Who makes these things happen? Is there some kind of mechanism that runs ceaselessly, never allowing things to stop? Do clouds make rain, or does the rain make the clouds? The winds come from the north, now blowing east, now west, whirling high above the clouds. Are they somebody's breath? Who is huffing and puffing, making the winds whistle and the clouds move across the sky?

The wise ones tell us that heaven and earth follow their own nature. No one can make them do things that are unnatural to them. When sovereigns and leaders follow the natural turning of heaven, there will be peace and order. When they move against the turning of heaven, there will be disasters and social disorder. When a ruler shines like a mirror reflecting the natural ways, the world will support him and beckon to his call.

The most exalted are usually not interested in titles and renown. The most wealthy are usually not interested in riches. Those with the loftiest ideals are usually not interested in fame and reputation. The Way, like water, follows the lowest gradient. It naturally winds its way toward the bottom, seeping through hidden cracks and crevices, to disappear into oblivion.

Fame is a dreaded weapon—don't reach for it too often. Benevolence is like the home of the rich and powerful—don't stay for more than a night. The sage uses benevolence as a borrowed tool and employs integrity as a temporary shelter. Never tied to one place, she wanders in the lush forests as well as in the wastelands. She eats a simple meal in the fields of farmers and strolls in undecorated gardens. Free and easy, she rests in nonaction. Plain and simple, she finds life easy and fulfilling. Undecorated and dull, she does not have any wisdom to be displayed.

Those who believe in wealth will find it hard to give up their earnings. Those who value renown and recognition will find it hard to stay away from fame. Those who are attracted to power will hang on to leadership and never be able to hand the kingdom over to successors. Such people will not stop to reflect, let alone look at anything without wanting it. Clinging to the dichotomies of resentment and kindness, acceptance and rejection, giving and taking, punishing and being punished, and life and death, they shiver with fear, unable to accept the turning of events and the changing of fortunes. If you want to rest in simplicity, you must learn to move with the freedom of the wind and stand in the perfection of virtue. If you can't accept your place in the process of change, how can you expect to rule the world?

It was said that when the Yellow Emperor performed his music, his guest, a minister, said, "When I first heard the music, I was afraid. Then, hearing more, I felt weary of the world. By the end, I felt utterly confused and overwhelmed."

The Yellow Emperor replied, "I am not surprised you felt that way. First I performed the music through the eyes of humanity. Next I tuned into the movement of heaven. Finally I planted in it in the Great Clarity. Perfect music must first empathize with humanity and be rooted in virtue. Then it must be tempered by the march of heaven. Finally it must blend with clarity and spontaneity. Only then can the seasons turn in a timely manner; only then can the ten thousand things have a chance to grow. Soaring, sinking, flourishing, decaying—all are in harmony with the natural order. In this music, the clear notes blend with the dull, the rhythm of yin merges with that of yang, the sounds flow in tendrils like light, and silence hibernates like insects ready to wriggle again in spring. At the end, there is no tail; in the beginning, there is no head. Now emerging, now dissolving, always transforming, yet it is also unchanging in its constancy. This is what scared you.

"Then I played harmony with yin and yang," he continued, "illuminating the sound with the light of the sun and the moon. I made the notes long or short, soft or strong, modulating or in unison, yet never constrained by rules and form. In a valley, they filled the valley; in the void, they filled the void. They flowed into the crevices, held the spirit in the center, and accepted all things in their own terms. The tones were clear and radiant, the mood bright and clear. Ghosts and spirits were kept in their places; the sun, the moon, and the stars moved through their orbits. When the sound stopped, there was no end. When it started, there was no beginning. You were shown the emptiness of the Way, and you knew you could not describe its vastness. Your body and mind melted with the emptiness, and you were plunged into total freedom. It was this freedom that made you weary of the world.

"Finally," the Yellow Emperor concluded, "I tuned the music to spontaneity. Out of chaos sprang forms. Forms returned to the formless, disappearing into obscurity where there was no sound. The notes moved in no direction and rested in mysterious shadows. Sometimes it [the music] fell like death, sometimes it emerged like life. Sometimes it manifested as a flower, sometimes a fruit. Flowing, merging, disintegrating, it bowed to no one. You wanted to pin it down, but you had no way to grasp it. Music begins by evoking a fear of the unknown. The fear leads to dread. When I wove together dread and weariness, there was acceptance. When there is acceptance, I can end it by evoking confusion. With confusion, you are rattled to the core. When you are rattled, you will begin to feel stupid and simple. At this point you will be ready to be carried along the Way. This is the music of the turning of the heavens."

## CONSTRAINING FREEDOM

To be highbrow in everything you do, to be aloof from the everyday world, to shun its customs, to be sophisticated in discourse, and to be critical and snide—this is the lifestyle favored by the those who want to live in isolation. To condemn the world and its mundaneness, to feel wearied by the world, to be utterly despaired by what is happening around them—this is the mentality of those who want to end it all by plunging into the deep river. To preach benevolence, dedication, loyalty, and honesty; to have a sense of correctness in rites and rituals; to be moderate, modest, and polite—this is the lifestyle favored by those who want to educate the masses.

To talk about great achievements, to win fame and renown, to set down the rules and regulations of correct etiquette, to appoint people to positions and define their responsibilities, to ensure that the affairs of the state are running smoothly, to expand the territory of the nation by peaceful coexistence or conquest—this is the lifestyle favored by those who serve their country. To mend fences and clean ponds, to fish idly by the river, and to rest in nonaction—this is the lifestyle of the hermit-scholar who is uninterested in social and political engagements. To puff and expel the old breath and inhale the new, to imitate the postures of the bear and the bird, to be concerned only with cultivating the energy of life—this is the lifestyle of those who aspire to be like Peng Zu, who was said to have lived eight hundred years.

All these lifestyles constrain freedom by encouraging a tendency toward certain things and the avoidance of others. Limiting your options by constraining freedom or encouraging options by promoting freedom are just two sides of the same coin. Both are lifestyles that accept certain actions and reject others.

However, to have a vast view without constraining freedom, to be virtuous without having to be trained to be benevolent and loyal, to bring order to society without wanting fame and renown, to wander leisurely in the universe without being confined to the mountains and seas, to have a long life without exerting effort to attain it, to be comfortable with losing everything yet possessing everything, and to rest in the luminosity where all good things begin and end—this is what it means to follow the ways of heaven and earth and rest in the virtue of the sage.

Emptiness, stillness, clarity, simplicity, and nonaction are the pillars of heaven and earth and the foundation of virtue. The sage rests in heaven, on earth, and in virtue. With rest there is peace; with peace there is nonaction. In nonaction, worry and concern cannot touch him; in peace, the poisons of the world cannot harm him. Because his virtue is complete, his spirit is not confused.

In life the sage follows the ways of heaven and earth. In death she dissolves and merges with all things. In stillness she is at one with the virtue of yin; in movement she flows with the action of yang. She does not bring fortune or cause misfortune. She responds only when circumstances call for it. She acts only when it is necessary. She rises to the occasion only when there is no other alternative. Throwing away the whys and wherefores, she journeys through the ways of heaven, earth, and virtue.

Because the sage is at one with heaven, earth, and virtue, he never meets with disaster. Nor is he burdened by material things. He is not slandered by people or bothered by spirits. He floats with life and rests with death. He neither worries nor schemes. Like a light that does not dazzle, he is kind to everyone and everything. Completely trustworthy, he does not need to make promises. His sleep is dreamless, and his waking hours are free from worry. His spirit is pure and his soul is not tired. In emptiness, nothingness, and simplicity, he is in harmony with the natural order of heaven and earth.

Grief and elation pervert virtue, fear and anger obstruct the Way, and attraction and repulsion work against virtue. When you are without worry or expectation, virtue is complete. When there is oneness and constancy, stillness is complete. When there is no opposition to anything, emptiness is complete. When there is no resentment, purity is complete.

If the body works too hard and does not rest, it will weaken. If generative energy is used without restraint, it will be exhausted. If energy is depleted, you will feel tired. It is the nature of water to be clear if it is not mixed with dirt. If water is not stirred, it will remain still. Dam it, and it will not flow. If it stops flowing, it will no longer be clear. Such is the nature of the ways of heaven and earth.

If you remain pure and simple, you will not be confused. To be still, clear, and nonintrusive; to move along the celestial path of the sun, the moon, and the stars—this is the essence of cultivating the spirit. The spirit extends to the four directions. Above, it touches the sky; below, it embraces the earth. It transforms and nourishes all things, but its form cannot be grasped. The way to colorless purity and clarity is to not let them wander away. When you are never separate from the spirit, you are at one with its essence. The common person values gain, the person of integrity values reputation, and the person with ability values motivation and aspirations. The sage, however, values the spirit.

Colorless means white, and whiteness means there is nothing mixed in. When there is nothing mixed in, we say it is pure. When spirit is pure, it is not confused. Those who embody purity and transparency are called True Beings.

## TRYING TO REPAIR INBORN NATURE

Those who hope to attain clarity and return to the Source by trying to repair or enhance inborn nature through petty knowledge, and those who give excuses for desires, are deluded and blind.

The wise ones who followed the Way used tranquillity and equanimity to cultivate true knowledge. They abided in this knowledge and did nothing. They knew that true knowledge and stillness enhanced each other. As a result, harmony and order naturally emerged from their inborn nature. Virtue is harmony; the Way is order. When virtue is not separated from action, there is benevolence without pretense. When the Way is followed, there is honor and integrity. When honor and integrity are understood, there is loyalty. When there is purity within, the primal order is appreciated. When there is trust in thought and action, elegance is the norm. When respect is part of everyday life, rites and rituals emerge naturally.

The sages of old lived in the midst of the mundane and the chaotic. Existing with the rest of the world, they embraced simplicity and rested in silence. During those times, yin and yang were harmonious; ghosts and spirits did not wreak havoc; the seasons changed naturally; water, rocks, and trees were not harmed; and living beings did not die premature deaths. The wise ones had knowledge but did not use it. They had wisdom but did not force things along. As a result, all things came and went spontaneously, according to their own nature. When it was time for them to emerge, they were born without fanfare; when it was time for them to die, they dissolved without struggling.

When the way of virtue began to decline, people thought they needed to repair inborn nature. As a result, all kinds of plans to repair virtue emerged. Purity and simplicity were destroyed, and virtue became synonymous with conduct, protocol, and good behavior. People no longer trusted their inborn nature. They began to replace virtue with knowledge, hoping that knowledge and skills could bring order to the world. When they found that knowledge alone didn't do much, culture was introduced, mixed with breadth of learning.

Learning then bred arrogance, which led to debates of whose culture was best. Obsession with learning clouds clarity. With time, people lost clarity, they got confused and deluded, and they had no inkling of how to return to the Way. As a result, the world lost the Way. The Way was no longer part of the world, and both rapidly moved farther and farther apart.

What did the sages do in the face of all this? Although they did not always retire onto the mountains and into the forests, their virtue was hidden. Although they did not conceal themselves in caves and deep valleys, their wisdom was drawn inward. Although they did not actively refuse to use their abilities and talents, their knowledge was locked away. If destiny allowed, they would exercise virtue, wisdom, knowledge, and skill. If the times were not right, then all that was left for them to do was to deepen their roots, rest in truth, keep themselves alive, and wait.

How do you live in tumultuous times? First, do not decorate knowledge with ornaments. Second, do not use knowledge to make trouble or try to use it to repair virtue. Third, be true to your inborn nature and rest in vastness. Virtue has no use for petty understanding. Small mind turns you away from virtue, and petty understanding steers you from the Way. In this manner you will find fulfillment. When the sages spoke of fulfillment, they did not mean having material wealth or fame and recognition. For them, fulfillment meant that their lives were so joyous and complete that nothing could make them better.

## AUTUMN FLOODS

When the autumn floods arrived, the lord of the river was very pleased with himself, thinking that he was the greatest body of water on earth. But when the river reached the sea, the river lord, seeing the wide expanse of the waters, was humbled. Having seen the vast and limitless sea, he understood that it is impossible to weigh and measure everything. Time, permanence, and even space are all illusions.

The wise ones know that there is no beginning and no end. Observing that which is far and that which is immediate, the sage does not consider the large to be cumbersome and the small to be minuscule. She has a clear understanding of past, present, and future and prefers not to ponder whether time is long or short. Seeing the true nature of things, she is beyond fullness and emptiness, gain and loss. Walking the middle path, she is not interested in seeking either the high or the low. For these reasons, she does not exalt in life and does not dread the coming of death.

The realized ones do not harm others in their actions, nor do they display benevolence or charity. They see no reason to avoid the wealthy or to demean the porter at the gate. They do not scheme to attain wealth, but they do not refuse it when they receive it. They do not force people to help them, but at the same time they do not brag about being self-sufficient. In fact, when offered help, they happily accept it. Although their actions are different from those of the petty and the vulgar, they do not display eccentricity or aloofness. They are content to stay with the crowd but do not despise those who rush ahead. Fame and renown do not stir them to action, and punishments do not deter them from being true to virtue. Those who follow the Way win no fame; those who possess the highest virtue win no fortune. The realized ones have nothing to gain or lose because they have no notion of accomplishment or attainment.

Do not imprison your inborn nature by latching onto notions of few and many. Few and many are merely part of the natural coming and going of things. Be unbiased and humble like the earth. Soil and dirt do not grant special favors. Be expansive and broad-minded like the four directions. Directions know no bounds and limits. The Way is without form and limit and without beginning and end. That which has form will always have a beginning and an end. One moment, these things come into existence; another moment, they dissolve into nothingness. You can never find fulfillment in forms. Birth, growth, death, and decay are all part of the natural order of things. Hang on to any one of these, and you'll forever be confused.

Understand the Way, and you will have insight into the natural course of things. Know how things run their natural course, and you will be able to deal with emerging and dissolving circumstances. Know the principles of coming and going, and you will never be harmed. Embrace virtue, and you will not be harmed by fire, water, and wild animals. This has nothing to do with having magical abilities. It's about being able to intuitively distinguish danger from safety. Be content and do not force yourself beyond your limits. In this way, you will never get yourself into situations that will injure you.

If you understand that virtue is part of the Way, you will not let what is unnatural to the Way bury your inborn nature.

## TRUE JOY

Wealth, renown, and long life are what most people want today. Happiness is defined as a life of leisure, exotic food, fine clothing, beautiful sights, and pleasing sounds. Poverty, feeling useless, and an early death are what most people hate. A hard life with little rest, food without taste, clothing that is out of style, and no sights and sounds to entertain the senses are the things most people dread.

People who can't get fame and fortune will go to no end to attain them, and those who have them are deathly afraid that they will lose them. What a stupid way to live! Those who are rich spend their time trying to get richer, wearing themselves out by piling up more wealth than they can ever use. What a waste of time! Those who have a reputation and a name to uphold spend their time scheming to become more famous, afraid that others will see and exaggerate their small faults. What a useless way to spend energy! If you are worrying and fretting all the time trying to get more, you'll end up with a tired body and an addled mind, even if you live a long life. What a callous way to treat yourself!

True joy lies in nonaction. True joy knows no happiness or sadness; it is beyond praise or blame. Right and wrong are not decided by public opinion. If you measure yourself by what others think, you will live only to please the crowd. Since you can't please everyone, you will never truly be content and happy. Heaven follows the way of nonaction, letting things run their natural course. Its inaction is called purity. Earth also follows the way of nonaction, letting things come naturally to their own fruition. Its inaction is called peace. Heaven and earth are not interested in making things happen, yet things happen. Mysteriously, wonderfully, things emerge, are transformed, and then dissolve. All this happens without anyone deciding what should happen and what shouldn't happen. Leaving all things to mind their own business and not getting involved in the dirty work of twisting and turning fate and destiny—is this not true joy?

## ATTAINING LIFE

Those who understand what it means to attain life do not labor over the limits of life. Those who understand the true nature of destiny do not labor over what knowledge cannot change. If you want to nourish life energy, you must not dissipate it. At the same time, you must not be too attached to prolonging it beyond its limits. The coming of life cannot be manipulated, and its departure cannot be stopped.

If you want to nourish the body, first break the attachment to worldly things. Without entanglements, you can calmly follow the course of life naturally and won't always try to make things go your way. The breaking of attachments is important to cultivating life energy because if you are no longer worked up over gain and loss, you will not force your body to labor beyond its limits or squander your vitality trying to conquer the world. Your body will be in tune with the rise and fall of the vapors of heaven and earth. Consequently, their vapors and yours will freely exchange. When their vapors are absorbed into your life force, you will be free from illness.

The realized ones can stay under water and not drown, walk on fire and not get burned, and wander through creation without fear because they guard the true breath by resting within the limitless. Wandering freely between the beginning and the end of things, they nourish the breath, unite it with virtue, and join it with the source of creation. Protecting what belongs to heaven and embracing what belongs to earth, their spirit is pure and without blemish. How can fire, water, hope, or fear injure them?

If the vital breath is dissipated and not replenished, life energy will be depleted. If it rises but does not fall, this will lead to irritability. If it descends but does not ascend again, this will lead to forgetfulness. And if it neither ascends nor descends but simply hovers around the region of the heart, illness will result.

Realized beings wander beyond the dust of the world, roaming freely and aimlessly. They practice the art of doing but not forcing and caring but not bossing. In this way they preserve vitality, life, and virtue.

Don't try to develop what is created by force and unnaturalness. Let things run their own course naturally and effortlessly. Those who cultivate the Way will nourish life; those who push things stubbornly will injure life. If you don't reject heaven, don't harm earth, and don't neglect humanity, you'll be pretty close to the Way.

## MOUNTAIN TREE

There was a huge tree standing in a mountain forest. Its trunk was gnarly, its branches were thick, and its leaves were lush. A woodcutter passing by took one look at the tree, then decided not to touch it. Zhuangzi, who happened to witness this scene, asked the woodcutter why this giant tree was not harvested. The woodcutter replied, "This tree is useless. Its trunk is so ugly that nobody would want to make it into furniture. The branches are too big for firewood, and there are just too many leaves that need to be stripped." Zhuangzi commented, "Because of its worthlessness and ugliness, this tree will live out the span of life it was given."

If a tree is not felled because of its uselessness, how much can you live out your life without getting into trouble if you are quiet, aimless, and drifting? Climbing the Way and following virtue, neither praised nor blamed, now a dragon and now a snake; never holding to one course but always changing with the circumstances; and treating things as things but not letting yourself be treated as a thing—this will allow you to live out your days in peace.

It is natural for things to come together and then fall apart. That which is sharp will become blunted, those who hold high positions will fall, and the ambitious will eventually be defeated by their ambition. If you have some intelligence, you'll be the target of schemes; if you're stupid, you'll be cheated. Either way, you'll get eaten alive by plots and intrigues. Only when you follow the Way and walk in virtue will you not come to harm.

Animals with beautiful fur will be killed for their pelts. No matter how well they hide, they'll be caught eventually. They may stay in their lairs during the day, venturing out to hunt only at night. Yet one day, they'll walk into nets and traps. It's not because these animals are not cautious or that they are unlucky. The fact is that their beautiful fur is killing them. In the same way, those who wear knowledge as an elegant garment are also in danger of being in harm's way. Strip away your elegant robe of knowledge. Rid yourself of your beautiful coat of abilities. Dwell in emptiness and clarity. Be simple; blend within the dust and dirt of the world, and you'll never be noticed.

There is a country where people are simpleminded and unsophisticated. Not knowing what it means to desire, they are not preoccupied with getting what they want and losing what they have. They know how to give things away but don't look for anything in return. They are courteous to one another but know nothing of etiquette, rites, and rituals. Unadorned and unrestrained, they wander aimlessly in the vast expanse—this is what it means to follow the Way. When there is a birth, they rejoice; when there is a death, they prepare a fine funeral. Accepting that life and death are part of the natural way of things, they do not desire to lengthen their lives by taking herbs and minerals. Nor do they shorten their lives by throwing away their life energy.

If you wish to live in such a country, you should discard your name and break away from those things that strain your body and tire your spirit. Let the Way be your guide and journey there. Let unconventionality be your helper. Let an unfettered mind be your vehicle. Lessen your needs, minimize your desires, don't make too many detailed plans, don't harbor too many expectations, and you'll get there. You may have to cross endless mountains and valleys and drift across wide-open oceans. Even though you gaze as far as you can, you may never see your destination. Those who come to see you off will stay behind as you move farther and farther into the distance.

You may think that the journey to this hidden land is fraught with hardship. But hardship exists only for those who worry too much. Those who wander through the Great Silence always travel alone, effortlessly and aimlessly. When you're done with all the carving and polishing that has to be done, return to the simplicity of the uncarved block. Happily bid farewell to what goes; joyfully greet that which comes. For what comes cannot be denied, and what goes cannot be stopped.

Boasting about success means you have failed. True success need not be broadcasted. Therefore, let go of success, fame, and recognition and mingle with the common and the ordinary. The Way flows far and wide in realized beings, but they are not attached to its brightness. Their virtue moves effortlessly, but they do not dwell in renown. Like bears they wander aimlessly in the forest, shrugging off their power, wiping off their paw prints to leave no trails. Thus, they have no cause to blame others, and others have no reason to blame them. Leisurely they walk in a free and easy manner. They gave away their learning, sat in silence, and returned to simplicity. Their students no longer come seeking wisdom. Officials no longer come patronizing their talents. But their affection and friendship are greater than ever.

It is best to leave the body relaxed. When feelings emerge, it is best to let them come and go. When you go along with things rather than fight them, you will not run the risk of becoming their enemy. By keeping your body relaxed, you will avoid getting fatigued. By letting your feelings come and go, you won't dissipate life energy. And when you are not at odds with the world and are not fatigued by worrying about everything, you'll find no need to bask in luxury, seek reward, or depend on things going your way. When you embrace virtue but cannot apply it, you need not be distressed.

Wait for the right time, and you'll be able to serve humanity. If you're poor, unknown, and unnoticed, you should not be distressed. Hunger, thirst, cold, heat, and discomfort are all part of life and the natural turning of events. Humanity exists because of the Way, and the Way exists because of itself. Humanity can never cause the Way to exist because humanity is limited, whereas the Way is limitless.

The tree with an unblemished trunk will be the first to fall and be made into beams and pillars. The well that is brimming with sweet water will be the first to run dry. And those who show off their learning and abilities to impress others, who display and wear their virtue like a colorful shirt, and who go around parading good deeds like bright lights will be the first to fall. The sage simply plods along effortlessly. In life he is never prominent; in death he does not leave a trace. He understands his coming, embraces the changes, and accepts his going with calmness and fortitude.

### TIEN ZIFANG

When a man named Tien Zifang was asked why he never praised his teacher or talked about him, he replied, "There's nothing extraordinary about my teacher. He's a human being with the heart of heaven. He follows the Way, keeps true to virtue, and embraces all things. If he encounters those who do not follow the Way, all he has to do is be himself, and the ignorant will become enlightened. If all he does is to be true to himself, why is this extraordinary?"

Yin and yang are actually quite simple to understand. Ultimate yin is cold and stern; ultimate yang is warm and bright. The sternness and coldness of ultimate yin comes from the heart of heaven's yang. The warmth and brightness of ultimate yang comes from the heart of earth's yin. The essences of yin and yang are embedded in their opposites, so each already exists within the other. Yin and yang interact, copulate, commingle, and harmonize with each other, bringing forth all life. Birth, life, decay, and death all come to pass, but who manipulates this process? The sun shifts, the moon waxes and wanes—who's pulling the strings? Life has its beginnings, and death has its destination. Beginning and end follow each other in an unbroken cycle. This is simply the natural way of things.

When water dances and skips over stones and ledges, it is its nature, not something it does deliberately. It's the same way with the sage's relationship to virtue. Virtue is simply natural to her. She does not need to work hard at it or even cultivate it. It's as natural as the height of the sky and the depth of the earth, so what is there to cultivate?

The ones who embrace the Way are simple and ordinary. Therefore, gossipers leave them alone. Plain and unassuming, they do not arouse interest. Dull and silent, they do not invite debate and argument. While many regard life and death as great events, these things have no hold over them. Because they are not threatened by changes or attached to titles and wealth, their spirit can soar over the highest mountains and plunge into the deepest springs. Elevated, they are not arrogant; unnoticed, they are not distressed. Their fullness fills heaven and earth. They give everything to others, yet they possess all.

## KNOWLEDGE JOURNEYS NORTH

Knowledge journeyed north, ran into Do-Nothing, Say-Nothing, and asked for advice: "How can I find the Way? What path should I take? What kind of practices will I need to attain tranquillity?" Do-Nothing, Say-Nothing was silent. He didn't answer—not because he did not want to answer but because he simply did not know how to answer.

Undaunted, Knowledge kept going. He encountered Wild-and-Witless and asked the same questions. Wild-and-Witless said, "Yes, I can give you the answers." But just as he was about to open his mouth, he promptly forgot what he was supposed to say.

Failing to get any answers, Knowledge returned home and paid a visit to the Yellow Emperor, who was known to be the wisest man of his time. "How can it be that these sages don't even have a clue on attaining tranquillity and clarity, when you and I sometimes have a vague idea of what we should do?" asked Knowledge.

The Yellow Emperor replied, "Do-Nothing, Say-Nothing got it. Wild-and-Witless appeared to get it. You and I, however, are nowhere near being right. Those who know do not speak, and those who speak do not know. You can't talk about the Way or force its virtue. However, you can cultivate and practice benevolence, kindness, and generosity. You can also talk about integrity, honesty, honor, and humility and figure out better ways to apply them. When humanity distanced itself from the Way, it also abandoned virtue. When it abandoned virtue, there was a need to promote benevolence, kindness, and generosity.

"When even these acts are dismissed," he continued, "what we have left are laws, protocols, and rituals. When even those are gone, we have disaster on our hands. Those who follow the Way do less and less each day. Finally they end up doing nothing and saying nothing. However, because nothing is said and nothing is done, everything is done."

Knowledge said to the Yellow Emperor, "Why do you say that Do-Nothing, Say-Nothing was right on the mark, Wild-and-Witless was off, and we were downright wrong?"

The Yellow Emperor replied, "Do-Nothing, Say-Nothing was correct because he honestly did not know and admitted it. Wild-and-Witless appeared to be correct because he thought he knew but then forgot it. We were wrong because we thought we knew."

Life is the beginning of death, and death is the beginning of life. Who can understand the workings of heaven and earth? Life is simply the emergence of breath. When breath emerges, there is life. When breath stops, there is death. Life and death are a matter of the appearance and disappearance of breath. Since life and death follow each other, why be anxious about their coming and going? All things come from the Source. We judge some to be beautiful and worthy and others to be ugly and useless. But in an instant, things that are beautiful can become foul, and those that are useful can become worthless. The sage knows that there is only one breath coming from one Source. Therefore, he always values this oneness.

Heaven and earth have great beauty, but they never talk about it. The seasons are clear about their timeliness, but they do not discuss it. The myriad things follow the principles of birth, growth, and dissolution, but they do not expound on them. Not acting, not moving, they perceive the workings of heaven and earth, join with the purity and brightness of the Way, and are at one with the transformations of all things. Living or dead, square or round, hard or soft—no one knows how things got that way.

There is nothing in the world that does not change. Night and day, and spring, summer, autumn, and winter, follow each other naturally. The Way—dark, hidden, and mysterious—seems not to exist but is always lurking there. Rich and limitless, it possesses no form, yet its spirit pervades all things. The myriad things are guided by it, although they do not know how and why. We call it the root of all things, or the Source.

To stay rooted in the Source, straighten up your body, clear your vision, and be in harmony with everything under heaven. Draw in your knowledge, be regal and confident in your bearing, and let the spirits guide you. Beautify your life with virtue, let the Way be your home, be pure as a newborn animal, and don't try to find reasons for everything. Use simplicity to guide your life, clear your mind of impurities, and wash and purify your spirit. Let your body be still like earth. Dissolve yourself into oblivion. Stay true to the fundamental reality and don't search for answers. Rest in the dim, dark grotto. Then you will naturally be rooted in the Source.

Your body is a form that the Source lent you when you were born. You don't own it, just as you don't own your destiny and inborn nature. You don't even own your children or your wealth—if you own them, why are you forced to leave them behind when you die? Therefore, it's best to walk and not be concerned with where you're going. Work without making things happen, and rest without thinking too much about it.

The Way is bright and luminous, shining out of deep darkness. Order emerges from chaos. Form appears out of the formless. The pure spirit is born of the Way. All things owe their lives to the Way; all come from the Source. We don't know where they came from and where they will go. The Way has no gate. It is an open and wide road leading to the four directions. Those who walk it will be strong in limb, keen in intellect, and wise in judgment. Unbiased and free from prejudice, they will respond to things without acceptance or repulsion. They know that it's natural for the sky to be high, the earth to be broad, and the seasons to change. Breadth of learning does not necessarily mean knowledge; a good command of knowledge does not necessarily entail wisdom.

Thus the sage is not concerned with acts of increasing and decreasing. That which increases will increase without showing signs of waxing, and that which decreases will wane unannounced. The sage holds on to that which is deep and unfathomable like the sea and that which is high and lofty like the mountains. For a brief time, she is mortal, and then she will return to the Source. Her life is simply the gathering of breath, and her death is a departure of breath. It is natural for trees to bear fruits, vines to climb, and flowers to spread pollen. It is also natural for human relationships to form and dissolve. The sage, encountering these things, does not go against them or cling to them. To respond to them naturally, without praising or condemning, is virtue. To embrace them in fellowship is the Way.

The formless is the basis of forms. Form emerges from the formless, and form returns to the formless. This is a truth that we need to arrive at without conception. Trying to reach this conclusion by debating and searching for evidence does not work. Those who pontificate and expound the facts will not reach it, and those who have reached it will find no need to argue about it. Those who look with expectation will not see it. Those who speak elegantly of it will only cloud its existence.

The Way cannot be seen or heard. It emerges only in stillness and silence. Join with me in quietude, harmony, leisure, and inaction, and you will never experience exhaustion. I go nowhere and arrive without knowing how far I've traveled. I come and go and never think about starting and stopping. I've been everywhere and back, but I don't know if the journey is completed. I relax and wander freely in the vastness. Knowledge enters, and I am not aware of its existence. Wisdom enters, and I don't know where it begins or ends.

If you treat things as objects, you will always be limited by "objectness." If you move beyond the realm of fixity and limits, you will enter the realm of the limitless. The Way fills and empties the ten thousand things, but it is never filled or empty. It makes things grow and wither, but it itself is never subjected to maturation and decay. It allows roots to dig deep and branches to spread wide, but it itself does not have roots and branches. It stores and scatters but has no idea of storage and scattering.

People in ancient times changed according to changes in nature. People nowadays play around with thoughts, trying this idea and that, sometimes adopting kindness, sometimes meanness, but stay fixed in their minds despite changing conditions. This is no way to live. The sage lives with others but does not harm them. Those who don't harm others will not meet with harm themselves. We delight in having a good home and family and a decent livelihood. Loss of loved ones, home, and possessions grieves us. The sage does not deny that these feelings are aroused naturally; it's just that he does not crave one and abhor the other.

Perfect speech is silence. Perfect action is nonaction. Perfect understanding is not knowing you understood. To limit your understanding only to that which can be understood is shallow and ignorant indeed!

# 14

# The Miscellaneous Chapters

## GENGSONG CHU

Gengsong Chu was an attendant of Laozi's who managed to learn some things about the Way from the sage. After Laozi departed, Gengsong Chu went north and lived in a remote mountain valley. He kept to himself but occasionally got help from the local villagers, who were considered stupid and idle. After three years of his living there, the villages in the area prospered. The crops multiplied, the livestock was healthy, and there was no crime. The village elders suspected that it was Gengsong's influence, so they proposed to make him a deity and honor him with a shrine.

When Gengsong Chu heard about this, he immediately left. His friends thought this behavior strange, but Gengsong Chu said, "When spring comes, plants grow and flowers bud. When autumn comes, fruits ripen and the crops are ready for harvest. How could it be otherwise? The Way gets things going without anyone's interference. My staying here will only encourage those petty elders to set up sacrificial altars and make up rituals to complicate people's lives. I do not wish to be the cause of the villagers' misery."

Birds fly high to escape hunters; fish and turtles dive deep to stay away from nets. Similarly, to preserve the body and conserve life energy, we need to know how to hide, not minding other people's affairs and not encouraging them to weave rituals to complicate their lives. Rewarding worthy individuals and parading them around as models will only tempt people to push others to climb the social ladder. Allowing the learned to display knowledge will encourage people to argue for the sake of debating. Ambition does not make people ingenious; on the contrary, it makes them petty and argumentative. When ambitions go unchecked, people will work only for fame and profit. Family members will turn against one another, ministers will betray their sovereigns, merchants will cheat their customers, and neighbors will make war with one another.

The sage lives in the thick of humanity. She plows the earth for food and takes her leisure in the natural way of things. She does not get involved with petty rights and wrongs, or with profit and loss, and does not partake in the schemes and plots of politics. Unpredictable and unencumbered, she comes leisurely and goes freely. This is the basic principle of life preservation. Like a baby, she acts without knowing and wanders around with no destination in mind. She has no idea of beauty and ugliness or what should be considered good and bad. Because she does not manipulate the fortunes of others, no one can manipulate her.

Those who rest in tranquillity and clarity will emanate a radiant light. This light, however, is neither dazzling nor blinding. To people, these beings appear as people; to things, they appear as things. When you attain this state of being, others will naturally be drawn to your presence. Without actively commanding, you can rule the world.

To truly learn is to learn that which cannot be learned. To practice means practicing that which cannot be practiced. To be discerning means to discern that which cannot be discriminated. To understand means to rest in that which cannot be understood.

Nourish your body with the energy of life. Rest in thoughtlessness and give life to your consciousness. Honor your inborn nature and extend this to others. Know that there is a guardian who protects the house where your spirit dwells. If your protector is vigilant, nothing can enter to harm the spirit. Be sincere and honest with yourself, or you will be entrapped by petty concerns. Those who are not open and clear are vulnerable to materialistic attachments. If you have not done anything against your inborn nature, you will never fear that which lurks in the darkness. If you focus on what is within, you will not do good deeds for the sake of reward and recognition.

However, if you focus on material rewards, you'll only be concerned with hoarding goods. Those who do good deeds without any wish for wealth and recognition are called possessors of light because their deeds emanate the light of the spirit within. If you go along with the natural way of things, things will come to you. However, if you try to force your way through, you'll never have enough space for yourself and others. Those who have no room for others will find others threatening. In the end, these people can befriend no one, and no one can befriend them. Alienate yin and yang, and they will become your enemies. It's not that yin and yang will actively harm you; it's your confusion that makes them deadly.

People today think that independence is a desirable thing, that yin and yang should be completely separated to each maintain its own identity. They equate independence with separation and encourage people to promote their uniqueness instead of embracing the interdependency of all things. So they go about glorifying their independence, forgetting that all things come from the Source and are inherently connected to one another. They claim great discoveries only to realize in the end that they have wiped themselves out chasing illusions.

Those who analyze put knowledge on a pedestal. Using the authority of knowledge, they go about assigning right and wrong to every action. They consider themselves the arbiters of correctness, doling out rewards and punishments. They define what is wise and what is ignorant. Those who are considered wise are judged to be worthy; those who are considered dull are deemed unworthy. Those who are successful are rewarded with fame; those who fail are heaped with shame. This is what happens when analyzers dominate.

The most perfect ritual does not discriminate. If you step on a stranger's foot, you apologize; if you step on your brother's foot, you apologize even though you know he does not mind; if you step on your parent's foot, you apologize even though you know in your heart that you are forgiven. Those with perfect knowledge do not scheme, those with perfect benevolence show no outward affection, and those with perfect trust have absolute faith in the other.

Wipe out delusions generated by will, undo attachments that bind your heart, dissolve conceptual notions of what is virtuous and what is not, and you will clear obstacles to the Way. Renown, recognition, fame, authority, wealth, and profit are the six delusions of the will. Appearance, pedigree, facial complexion, handsomeness, charisma, and pride in the body are the six attachments that bind the heart. Repulsion, desire, elation, anger, grief, and happiness are the six snares of virtue. Rejecting, accepting, taking, giving, having know-how, and practicing tricks are the six obstacles to the Way. When these groups of six pitfalls no longer dwell within, you will naturally be virtuous. When you are virtuous, you will no longer be bullied by attachments. When attachments no longer rule you, you will be still. When you are still, your spirit will be bright. When your spirit is luminous, this is called enlightenment.

If you wish to be still, you must calm your energy. If you wish to nourish the spirit, you must still your thoughts. If you want your actions to have an effect, you must go along with the most appropriate thing to do. This is the way of the sage.

Virtue models itself after the Way, and life is the light of virtue. Inborn nature (of goodness) is the substance of life. When inborn nature moves, it is called right action. When it is still, it is called virtue. Action that is forced is called artificial action. An act that is done because it is the appropriate thing to do is virtue in action. Understanding that aims to analyze sees only schemes and plots. Understanding that aims only to understand is like a child's innocent wonder. Action and understanding that are not centered on self are called good order. This comes from being skilled in managing the affairs of humanity.

All things come from the Source and return to the Source. The Source has no form, yet it is the origin of all things. It transforms itself in time, yet it has no beginning and no end. There is a coming and a going, but there is no one setting these processes in motion. To enter the mysterious Source is to step into the void. It is in this deep, dark place that the sage hides. The understanding of the ancient ones went a long way. Some saw that things have never existed and that all forms of existence are inherently empty.

Some went farther and saw things exist as they are. Life and death are part of the natural way of things. When life emerges, we burst from the Source. When death occurs, we quietly return to the Source. Then there are those who have gone the farthest. They dwelled in the void, seeing the vastness as the head, life as the body, and death as the rump. How can the three be separated when they are all part of the same entity? I would sincerely love to call these people my friends!

## XU WUGUI

Xu Wugui was an eccentric who was introduced by his friend to the Marquis of Wei (early fourth century B.C.E.). When the marquis saw that Xu was dressed simply in the garb of a mountain recluse, he said, "You are known to be wise and learned. It's a pity you have to live a life of hardship in the mountains. Serve me, and I will give you all the comforts you'll ever want in life!"

Xu Wugui replied, "I am the one who should be comforting you! If you try too hard to fulfill your desires, you'll harm your inborn nature. However, if you force yourself to stay away from them, you will harm your senses. Either way you lose!"

Once the Yellow Emperor met a young horse herder who was reputed to be an immortal, and asked for advice on how to govern a nation. The boy replied, "I've never governed an empire. All I do is herd horses. I suppose governing a country is like caring for horses. Get rid of whatever is harmful to the horses, and they'll be healthy and contented." The Yellow Emperor bowed low and retired.

Scholars are not content if they do not spin ideas and thoughts. Debaters are not content if there is no argument and rhetoric. Examiners are not content if they cannot interrogate and intimidate. Trapped by the boundaries they've built, these people will never be exposed to the vast view. Those who want to win a high place in government will strive to bring attention to their achievements. Those who want to be praised for their skills and abilities will work hard at their duties at the cost of health and family. Those who want to appear brave will be willing to put their lives at risk on the battlefield.

Shabby artists want to display poverty to show that they are true to their art. Legislators crave more laws. Those who champion benevolence want to do away with bureaucracy. Farmers are not content to plow; they actually welcome weeds so that they can get rid of them. Merchants are not content to offer their goods at decent prices; they actually welcome haggling. Artisans are not content to create practical artifacts; they like to include useless features in their products. Greedy people can never be satisfied, because if they were, they would not have a chance to worry about what they can't get and what they would lose. Ambitious people feel threatened if there are no more challenges. The military feels uncomfortable if there are no wars. Those in power are afraid of peace and prosperity because it means they can no longer control the public by promising peace and prosperity.

All these people drive their minds and bodies day after day. What they get in the end is a sickly body and a tired mind. Drowned in the muck and mire they've created for themselves, they end their lives forever disconnected from the Way.

There are three groups of people who are at risk of losing body and mind: those who are smug, those who are loaded with burdens, and those who don't want to commit to anything. The smug are those who have learned the words of a teacher and can't wait to teach it. Pleased with a morsel of knowledge, they think their learning is vast, not realizing that they haven't even started to learn. Those who are burdened push beyond the limits of body and mind. They return home every day wiped out, not knowing how to replenish their life energy. Their senses are dim, their minds are confused, and their bodies are weak and ill. Those who are afraid to commit to anything don't know what's going on and don't know what to do with their lives. They find a place plagued with vermin with no water supply and call it paradise. They work in conditions where they could be promoted one day and fired the next and call it a dream job. Their advancement in the world is unpredictable, and their retirement yields no rest.

One who shares virtues with others is called a sage. One who serves others with one's abilities is called a worthy individual. If you use your skills to win praise and power over others, you will never have their loyalty. If you humble yourself, however, you will never lack support. The sage embraces heaven and earth. He does not need to hold a title or be appointed into a position to help. To those in need, he shares his fortune. To those in suffering, he offers compassion. In life he works without fanfare; in death he leaves no trace. The sage does what comes naturally to him, which is to apply virtue. In this way, he is no different from a dog that excels in guarding a house and barking at intruders, or a cat that excels in catching mice that raid pantries.

The sage pays no attention to what the crowd is doing. She neither seeks their approval nor distances herself from them. Embracing virtue, she finds harmony, pats her tummy, and rambles around freely. Use the eyes to select what you see, use the ears to choose what you should hear, and use the mind to restore clarity to the mind. The ancient ones used the principles of the Way to guide humanity; they never used the ways of humanity to direct the Way.

Those who are truly great do not think about doing something great. Those who are virtuous do not think about being virtuous. Heaven and earth are great, but they do not brag about their greatness. Those who understand what it means to possess greatness do not seek it, reject it, or change their ways to please the few who always complain. Resting in the greatness of heaven and earth rather than themselves, they embrace that which is inexhaustible and imperishable. This is what is meant by possessing great clarity.

When we walk, the foot treads on only a small part of the earth, but it is the untrod vastness of the ground that keeps us moving. Our understanding may be small, but if it is grounded in the vastness of the limitless, it is enough to keep us on the path of the Way. To understand the limitless, we need to understand the Great Unity, the Great Yin, the Great Vision, the Great Equality, the Great Method, and the Great Simplicity. Penetrate the limitless with the Great Unity, untangle it with the Great Yin, practice it with the Great Method, embody it with the Great Vision, hold it with the Great Simplicity, and end it with the Way. Follow that which is luminous, hide in that which is dark and dim, and return to that which is simple and unadorned.

## XE YANG

Xe Yang was an itinerant scholar who wanted a post in the court of the lord of Chu (a feudal state in the Zhou Dynasty). After several unsuccessful attempts in getting an interview, Xe Yang finally approached his friend Wang Guo, who was reputed to have some influence with the lord's inner circle. However, Wang Guo believed that another man, Kong Yuxui, would be more effective in arranging for Xe Yang to meet the lord.

When Xe Yang asked his friend what manner of man Kong Yuxui was, Wang Guo replied, "He fishes by the river in summer, gathers berries in the forests in spring, and wanders around as his heart wishes. In hardship, he's the kind of man who can make his family content; in affluence, he can make them not brag about their wealth. While he can make kings forget about their power, his presence is enough to inspire and guide them. This is because his approach to life is to move along with things rather than against them. In this way he effortlessly instills unity and harmony in others. Don't you think Kong Yuxui would be better than I in persuading the lord to give you an audience?"

Xe Yang finally understood Wang Guo's advice and asked no more about meeting the lord.

The sage transcends confusion and complications. Merged with all things, he knows no beginning and no end, no season and no time of day. The common person wants to ask everyone about everything from beginning to end and ends up blindly following the so-called teachers. The sage, however, has not even considered that there is a beginning or an end. He simply moves through the world effortlessly, at one with age and time, never rushing and never stopping. For him there are no thoughts of failure or success, no notion of completion and achievement. No wonder others can't figure him out or keep up with him!

People today don't know how to care for their bodies and their minds. Their attitudes and behavior are no different from those of border guards who bully travelers because it's the only way the guards can feel important and powerful. People turn their backs on virtue, ignore their inborn nature, and destroy the dignity of others. Slipshod in relating to virtue, they are easily trapped by desire and power. When small favors and gains appear, they hang on to them and lose sight of the good of all. In time they stifle themselves, becoming burdened by life instead of delighting in it. This is no way to live!

The wise ruler is quick to attribute success to others and considers with great care if someone is to be blamed for failure. Today, many people in positions of power are quick to praise themselves and slow to thank others for their efforts. They complicate things, and when things don't work out, they blame others and never themselves. They burden subordinates with responsibilities and punish them for not being able to fulfill them. They make small matters large, make easy projects difficult, and penalize people who cannot complete their assignments. They make learning difficult and then laugh at those who are struggling. They are never the first to complete a journey, but they are the first to ridicule those who do not finish. How can these kinds of leaders not exhaust a country's resources and put fear into people's hearts?

It is said that a lack of virtue leads to arrogance and delusion, a lack of courage leads to closed-mindedness, a lack of strength leads to reliance on gadgets, a lack of knowledge leads to deceit, and a lack of contentment leads to theft.

When things enter your consciousness, there should be a host to receive them but never to cling to them. When thoughts emerge from consciousness, they should be guided but not constrained. Day and night follow each other; the seasons run their course; this is not because someone forces them to behave in this way, it's because it is part of the natural way of things. So it is with ruling a country. The leader of a nation is not partial to any of the departments or ministries and never seeks to control them. The departments do what is naturally their responsibility and are not subject to the whims of those in power. In this way, the functioning of the state will be well-ordered.

In this way, virtue is complete. The myriad things of the world differ from one another in function, but the Way does not favor one over the other or try to control them. If a ruler does not favor one minister or one subject over another, people will be content to be nameless. Being nameless, they can rest in nonaction. Resting in nonaction, they are effortless in everything they do and do not do. Being effortless, they can wander freely in the vastness of the void.

The Way is neither a being nor a nonbeing. We give it a name temporarily because that gives us a convenient way to talk about it. If you talk about it in conjunction with virtue, what you say will be relevant to the Way. If you talk about it with disregard to virtue, what you say will be words without much meaning. Neither words nor silence can do full justice to the teachings of the Way. To not think about it or talk about it, or even consider being silent about it, is the highest form of discourse.

## EXTERNAL THINGS

Rub two pieces of wood against each other, and you will spark a flame. Place metal into a fire, and it will melt. When yin and yang are unbalanced, sky and earth will go awry. In the same manner, when happiness and sadness run amok in our lives, we will become anxious and fearful. Our minds will be dangling in suspension between success and failure, acceptance and rejection. Gain and loss rubbing against each other can only generate fires that burn up inner peace and harmony. This is what happens when external things take control of us.

If you are able to wander aimlessly, how can anything keep you from being bogged down? However, if you are unable to let go, how can you even begin to think of being free? A mind that is tied down by conformity, a will that is bent toward aloofness, and an attitude that is anchored by an unwillingness to change are all incompatible with wisdom and virtue.

A penetrating eye sees clearly, a penetrating ear hears clearly, a penetrating nose smells clearly, a penetrating mouth tastes clearly, a penetrating consciousness perceives clearly, and a penetrating wisdom understands virtue clearly. The ability to penetrate is nothing more than not allowing the senses and the mind to be choked by external things. When we swallow too much food, we choke. When we take in too much sight, sound, smell, or taste, we get confused. When we are bombarded with too many thoughts, we get deluded. Too much stimulation will lead to disorder, and disorder harms not only ourselves but also other living things.

All things with consciousness owe their existence to breath. However, if they don't care about this life-giving breath, it is not the fault of heaven and earth. On the contrary, heaven and earth have endowed us with the ability to inhale life-giving breath and expel noxious airs. Nowadays, however, most people choose to block up the passages and close the doors instead. The body is like a building with many levels and rooms. If the levels are organized and the passages between them are unobstructed, we can wander from one room to another without constraint. However, if the rooms are small and the corridors are filled with furniture and junk, we will feel claustrophobic and edgy.

So it is with consciousness. If consciousness is a large space, we can wander around aimlessly; if consciousness is narrow and confined, we will never have the chance to wander. With time, we will become comfortable with living in a small mind and be afraid of venturing out to the wide world. If consciousness cannot be given free rein, the breath of life will not flow properly. Consequently, the internal organs will be malnourished, the senses will fight one another, and the body will collapse and die.

Forests, mountains, rivers, and lakes grow to be majestic without aiming to please. Trees grow tall and flowers bloom without any desire for display. Today, people love to show off their learning and abilities: they teach because they want to show off their knowledge, they clothe their teachings with sensationalism because they want to attract fame and wealth, they help because they want to be recognized, and they give because they want to be praised. Therefore, schemes blossom in times of crisis, knowledge sprouts in times of contention, stubbornness arises from fear of change, and government policies are made to please the mob.

If only humanity can return to the Way! Government policies will then be like spring rain: timely, appropriate, and nourishing. Knowledge and teachings will be like the autumn harvest: abundant, bountiful, and filling and nourishing the belly of the mind. People will not need to ask the learned ones how to live better lives. The learned ones will not need to get advice from the virtuous ones on how to change society for the good. And the wise ones will not need to ask the worldly ones how to get along with the times.

## WORDS THAT CARRY AUTHORITY

What kind of words carry authority? Certainly not those used by parents defending the wrongdoings of their children. No one expects these words to carry weight, because parents will always speak in favor of their children. If a nonrelated person advocates for those children, that argument will always appear more unbiased. This has nothing to do with whether the parents are truthful. It's because of how the public perceives it to be. These days it is sad that people value public opinion over virtue. A virtuous judge will deliver justice regardless of whether a defendant is an offspring or a stranger.

The words of those who are perceived as wise will carry authority. It is not because these people actually have wise things to say. Rather, it's because whatever they say is expected to be valuable. Old people who have not grasped the Way are still ignorant of the Way, no matter how much they have experienced life. They may be seniors, but they are just a remnant of the past. True authority is conveyed not because a person speaks loudly, frequently, or claims seniority. Words of wisdom are grounded in virtue. If you are virtuous, you will always speak from virtue, and in doing so, your words will carry authority.

The ten thousand things come from the Source, although they have different form and function. This is called the Great Equality. The Great Equality is part of the natural way of things. It is not something decided and agreed upon by scholars and debaters. Arguing with logic that things are equal does not make them equal. Manipulating logic to declare that things are not equal does not make them unequal. Promulgating decree that things are equal or unequal does not make them so.

When we start thinking too much, our minds become dead. When people strive too hard for public causes, forcing others to believe what they believe, their path in life becomes petty and confused. Heaven and earth have their own cycles of change. To be in harmony with heaven and earth is to follow the Way without striving. However, to live in the light of the Way is to have no path at all.

## GIVING AWAY THE THRONE

The sagely emperor Xun (before 2500 B.C.E.) wanted to give away the throne when he saw that his people were prospering and living harmonious and peaceful lives. Deciding that his work was done, he looked for successors to inherit the kingship. This was a man who had an inkling of what it means to follow the Way.

When Xun approached Zizhou and asked him to take the throne, Zizhou replied that his health was not good and that he needed to take care of his ailments before he could even think about ruling a kingdom. This was a man who valued his life force and would never exchange his health for fortune and power. He was well on his way to understanding the Way.

Xun next asked Shanquan to be his successor. Shanquan's answer was "I wander in the midst of space and time. In winter I dress in furs, in summer in hemp. To exercise my body, I plow in spring and harvest in autumn. In winter I rest my body and clear my mind, dining on what I have stored from the autumn harvest. I rise with the dawn and rest with sunset. I wander freely between heaven and earth." With this, Shanquan went deep into the mountains and was never seen again. This was a man who had almost embraced the Way.

Xun then asked his friend, a farmer of Stone Door village, to take the throne. The farmer simply lifted his wife onto his back, took his son by the hand, and, without a word, disappeared to the islands across the sea, never to return. This was a man who had never been separated from the Way.

The sage respects life and knows what it means to nourish the body and tame her desires. If she is rich and honored, she does not let wealth and power injure her clarity. If she is poor and unknown, she does not let concerns of fortune and fame entangle her body and muddle her mind. Today, people who occupy high offices in government or business are deathly afraid that they will lose their power and fortune. Fixed on profit and loss, fortune and misfortune, they risk their lives to get what they don't have and to keep what they have. They end up with a sick and tired body and a confused and deluded mind. Is this worthwhile?

The states of Han and Wei were once fighting over a small piece of territory along their border. The Marquis of Han asked the sage Huazi for advice. Huazi said, "If Wei tells you that the territory can be yours if you cut off your left hand, would you sacrifice your hand for a piece of land?" The marquis immediately replied, "Of course not. I would not want to lose my hand even for a piece of land."

Huazi then said, "You just acknowledged that your hands are more important to you than territory. And if your hands are valuable to you, how much more important is your body? If you value your body, you won't think about endangering life and limb going to war with your neighbor. If everyone weighed in on what is more important to them, their lives or their possessions, we'd be content with what we have and would not go to war."

The marquis replied to Huazi, "Of all the advice I've gotten, yours was the most enlightening!" The teachings of the Way lie in preserving and respecting life. When there is energy to spare, it can be used to manage the family and the state. If you use all your time and energy to conquer a country or take over a corporation, you won't be able to care for your life. Yet there are many today who would willingly sacrifice their health and sanity to pursue wealth, fame, and power. Would you willingly exchange a piece of fine jade for a broken shard of pottery?

There was a man named Xuanxian in the state of Lu who lived in a small house with a leaky roof and a broken fence. Yet he sat on a grass mat in a dignified manner and played his lute and sang. When his friend Zigong, who held a high position in government, visited him, Xuanxian came out to greet his friend wearing a hemp robe and straw sandals.

Zigong, seeing the sorry state his friend was in, tried to comfort him, but Xuanxian simply said, "I've heard people say that if you lack wealth, this is called poverty; if you've acquired learning but cannot put your knowledge to use, this is called distress. I may be poor, but I am not in distress. To pursue ambition by joining political parties, to study in order to show off learning, to teach in order to please your pride, to flatter in order to be promoted, and to abandon virtue to please the mob—I could not do these things. And that's why I may be poor but I am not in distress!"

Zigong was a student of Confucius. Although he held a high position in government, he had never been able to put what he had learned from his teacher into practice. Moreover, to preserve his position, he had to join cliques, flatter his superiors, and take part in court activities that were all show and no substance. Hearing his friend's comment, Zigong backed away, embarrassed, knowing that he could not part with his political career and social recognition. He might have been wealthier and more renowned, but he was also more distressed.

Another student of Confucius, Cengzi, lived in a wooden hut and farmed a nearby field. He wore a robe of hemp in summer and a coat of patched quilt in winter. He grew and harvested what he needed and never cut wood to light a fire. His hands were calloused from pulling weeds and planting grain, and his feet were hard from walking barefoot. Yet he would sing the old songs, greet the morning with joy, and go to bed without a care. The emperor offered him a position as a cabinet minister, but Cengzi refused. The feudal lords sent him gifts, but he returned them. Those who cultivate the spirit forget about profit and loss, those who nourish the body forget about fame and recognition, and those who walk the Way forget about the mind.

Yanzi was one of the most brilliant students of Confucius. Coming from a poor family, Yanzi was often persuaded by others, including Confucius himself, to seek employment in the civil service. Once, when Confucius again encouraged Yanzi to offer his services to the country, Yanzi said, "I have enough land near my home to farm for food and grow hemp for clothing. In my spare time, I study and play the lute. I am very happy and contented and have no desire to join the civil service."

Confucius's face was suddenly serious. In a soft and respectful voice, he said to his student, "You know contentment. Those who know what is enough will not be entangled by thoughts of gain, those who understand how to find satisfaction will not be afraid of loss, and those who cultivate what is within will never lose what is theirs. Even though they do not hold a political seat or become famous, they are not ashamed of their chosen lifestyle. I have tried to teach these principles to my students for a long time; you are the only one who not only understood but also practiced them."

Sages who embrace the Way are happy if they are shut in and happy if they can go out. It's not being shut in or being able to go out that makes them joyful. It's because, in embracing the Way, they see that being blocked or being let through is as natural as day and night, heat and cold, wind and rain. This is why some sages find enjoyment on top of a mountain, and others find contentment in a deep valley; some are happy to mingle with others, and others find satisfaction living as hermits.

## THE BANDIT CHI

There once was a notorious bandit named Chi who commanded a fierce band of followers. Handsome, daring, and shameless, he had what many desired: fame, fortune, and power. Today, people would say that to have good looks, wealth, and a commanding personality is the highest achievement in life. To be learned in many subjects and have the eloquence to talk about them would be the next highest achievement. To be brave, fierce, and determined and have a band of loyal followers at your side would be the lowest level of achievement.

Many would also say that someone who has all these achievements must be a person of virtue. If this were the case, we would consider the bandit Chi to be a virtuous man, since he was successful in everything he did. However, Chi got his wealth by robbing, stealing, and killing; he used his charisma to cheat and his good looks to obtain sexual favors. Moreover, he commanded his followers through fear and intimidation. Knowing this, would you consider Chi a virtuous man?

These days you can get rich if you are shameless, and you'll be trusted if you are famous. Your price, however, would be constant anxiety over how to present yourself to society and whether you could manipulate others. Having sleepless nights, worrying, being tired in body and mind—is this how you want to live? On the contrary, if you abandon reputation and gain, you will never have to think about being famous and shameless. Not tethered to profit and gain, renown and recognition, you will be able to embrace the Way and return to simplicity. Isn't this a better way to live?

The petty person will die for riches; the lofty person will die for reputation. Most people will consider the lofty person superior to the petty person. But these two are not that different. They both will not think twice about throwing their lives away for something external. So it is said, "Don't be a petty person; don't be a lofty person—return to your inborn nature, preserve your life, and follow the Way." Don't try to perfect your benevolence, don't risk your life for riches, and don't race after fame and reputation. If you need to make an effort to be benevolent, you are no longer benevolent. If you risk your life for wealth, you may get rich, but you'll forfeit your health and sanity. If you race after fame and reputation, you will forever be afraid of losing them. Anxiety over grief and sorrow and yearning for bliss and eternal joy bring no ease to the body. Fear and terror, elation and excitement, bring no clarity to the mind.

In times of trouble and disorder, would you remove yourself from the common lot, believing you are superior to the times, and watch the world go by your doorstep? Or would you mingle with the lowly and change as the world changes around you, believing that this is the best way to survive? Both ways are likely to ensure that you'll live a long life and not get into trouble. But you are far from the mark of being a follower of the Way.

When the wise ones decide to do something, it's always for the benefit of all. When there is enough, they do not try to get more. Having no reason to have more than what is necessary, they stop and retire into oblivion. If there is not enough, they will do whatever they can to make sure everyone has enough. If there is a surplus, they will give it away. Even if they gave away an empire, they would never consider themselves high-minded or altruistic. Greed and high-mindedness have nothing to do with setting the standard of ruling. In fact, they are a violation of the standard.

Rulers can command the power of leadership and yet not abuse this power. They can possess all the wealth of the kingdom yet not display their riches to mock and intimidate those who are destitute. When they take action, they calculate the risks and consider whether their behavior would harm others and injure their inborn nature. They may act or refrain from acting, but it is never for the sake of reputation or praise. The world may praise them, but they do not strive to do anything to gain the praises.

Contentment brings fortune, and excess brings harm. This is especially so with wealth. When you have a lot, you'll be likely to desire more. The ears will crave rich sounds, the mouth will crave the delicate flavors of meat and wine, and the body will crave sexual arousal and pleasure. This is called disorder. If you are drowned by uncontrollable passion, your life essence will be drained, and your body will feel like a mule carrying heavy loads uphill. This is called suffering. If you are greedy for riches, you'll work yourself to exhaustion. As a result, your body will be tired to the bone, and your mind will be addled and confused. At work you will be lethargic, and at home you will sink into languor—this is called disease.

If you search endlessly for wealth, you'll end up cramming your rooms with things you hoard but never use. Your house will be overflowing with objects, and your mind will be overflowing with thoughts, yet you will still desire more. This is called shame. If you don't know the difference between wants and needs, you will worry that you'll never have enough. This is called anxiety. If you are deathly afraid that your possessions will be stolen, you will install iron bars and padlocks in your home and refuse to travel without bodyguards. This is called terror.

Disorder, suffering, disease, shame, anxiety, and terror are the greatest weapons of destruction.

In the end, those who go after reputation will find it elusive. Those who seek gain and profit will find them impermanent. To trap the mind and tire the body in an endless pursuit of these things is called delusion.

## A DISCOURSE ON SWORDS

The king of the state of Wei was fascinated by swords and swordsmanship. He spent a lot of time testing and collecting swords from the finest smiths in his kingdom. As a result, he had little time to attend to the affairs of his country. The crown prince, concerned for the welfare of the citizens, wanted to find someone to persuade his father to devote time to governing the country rather than indulging in his hobby of swordsmanship. One of his ministers advised that Zhuangzi might be a good candidate for this task.

Zhuangzi accepted the prince's request and appeared before the king in the garb of a swordsman. Expecting a master smith and an expert swordsman, the first thing the king said to Zhuangzi was "What kind of swords do you make, and what expertise do you command in swordsmanship?"

Zhuangzi replied, "I make swords of all kinds. My workmanship is impeccable, and my skill has no rival. My blade displays the quality of emptiness. When drawn from the scabbard, it transcends fear and doubt. As for my skill, my sword will pierce my opponent first before he can touch me."

The king was very impressed and arranged for Zhuangzi to meet his best swordsmen. When Zhuangzi arrived at the tournament ground, the king said, "First tell me about the swords you plan to use."

Zuangzi replied, "I have brought three swords: the sword of the sovereign, the sword of the feudal lord, and the sword of the commoner. The sword of the sovereign is held in the scabbard of the four seasons. The five elements guide it, and the demands of honor and integrity direct it. Thrust it, and nothing can stand before it; lift it high, and there is nothing above; stab down with it, and nothing can block it; swing it, and nothing can hinder it. Above, it can cut through clouds; below, it can penetrate the deepest parts of earth. When you wield this sword, feudal lords will obey and respect you. Rebellions will be quelled without conflict, corruption will disappear, and the kingdom will enjoy peace, harmony, and prosperity."

The king was dumbfounded. After a brief silence, he asked about the sword of the feudal lord.

Zhunagzi said, "The sword of the feudal lord has wise and brave people as its point. Its blade consists of those who are pure of heart. People of trust and worth make up the spine. People of loyalty and dedication make up the sword guard. Heroes and fearless people make up the hilt. It too cuts without opposition from above, below, left, and right. This is because this sword is modeled after the roundness of heaven and the squareness of earth. When you slash with this sword, its arc follows the path of the sun, the moon, and the stars. When you stab with this sword, it follows the path of the four seasons. When it is used to command, it brings harmony and peace to the people. When the sword cuts, it is like the crash of lightning and thunder—corruption, pride, greed, and anger all melt away. Leaving fear, dread, doubt, arrogance, and pride dead in their paths, this sword will make all bow down and submit to virtue."

Finally, after much thought, the king said, "What about the sword of the commoner?"

Zhuangi replied, "The sword of the commoner is used by those with unkempt appearance, who swagger around looking fierce and aggressive. They slash each other to please the whims of the crowd. Above, it severs heads and necks. Below, it opens livers and lungs. When swung, it always draws blood. It has only one goal, and this is to cause maximal harm and injury. Those who wield this sword are no different from stray dogs fighting over territory. They have no place in the government of a kingdom."

Zhuangzi then bowed before the king and said, "May I be bold to say that Your Majesty has been using the sword of the commoner when you should be using the sword of the king. The discourse on swords is over, so I will now take my leave." With that Zhuangzi left the palace and was never found again.

After this incident, the king of Wei locked himself in his palace for three months to ponder Zhuangzi's discourse on the swords. When he emerged from the palace, he held in his hand the sword of the sovereign. His rough and undisciplined band of swordsmen had either left the country or committed suicide. The tournament hall and the training grounds were abandoned, the forges were cold, and no more weapons of destruction adorned the halls of the palace. Needless to say, the crown prince was very happy to see his father be a true sovereign again.

## THE OLD FISHERMAN

Once some students of Confucius met an old fisherman who asked what kind of work Confucius did and what manner of man he was. The students replied that Confucius taught people to practice benevolence; bring order to society through rites, rituals, and music; promote education for all classes of people; and live together in peace and harmony. The old fisherman merely nodded, then asked if Confucius owned an estate, ruled a fief, or held a position in government. When the students replied that their teacher never aspired to such ambitions, the old fisherman said, "Your teacher is definitely benevolent. But I am afraid he will still be unable to live out his years in peace. To tire body and mind in order to get people to follow rules and convention, to confine the natural ways within the boundaries of education, and to impose peace and harmony by leading citizens like a shepherd herding sheep—this is a vast distance from the Way."

When the old fisherman's words were reported to Confucius, the teacher exclaimed, "This man is a sage. I must visit him to learn more."

Confucius arrived at the old fisherman's hut, stood outside, announced himself, and said, "Honorable one, I have been enlightened by your remarks. Please advise me so I can benefit from your wisdom."

The old fisherman replied, "You are indeed humble and fond of learning. I, however, have nothing profound to teach. All I can say is the obvious. Since the beginning of time, creatures who follow the Way thrive; those who oppose the Way don't last long. Those whose duties are to mind the affairs of the state should mind the affairs of the state; those who are not appointed to do so should leave it to those who are.

"Making sure that there are enough taxes to repair roads, dams, irrigation ditches; that there is a system of just rewards and punishments; that corruption and favoritism are absent from the civil service; and that people with the right abilities are given the right tasks—these are the concerns of the high ministers," the old fisherman continued. "Making sure that your inner circle of advisers are loyal and benevolent, that your guards and soldiers are brave and skilled, and that you have collected enough taxes to make the annual tribute to the emperor—these are the concerns of feudal lords. Balancing yin and yang and making sure that the seasons are timely, that the rites and rituals are performed correctly, that the clans and feudal lords are harmonious, that the imperial silos are well-stocked, and that the neighboring countries do not invade you—these are the concerns of sovereigns. Now, you are not a feudal lord, a minister, or a sovereign. Why tire your body and mind by worrying over all these things?

"Do you know that there are eight pitfalls in life?" he asked. "They are the following: doing what you are not meant to do, rushing forward to do something recklessly, attributing qualities to those who are unworthy of them, speaking without regard to what is right or wrong, delighting in faulting others, breaking up friendships and relationships, using speech to slander or cause injury, and saying one thing and doing another. There are four great obstacles to virtue. These are plunging into great projects hoping to gain merit and fame, insisting that you know more than everybody else, seeing errors but refusing to change your ways, and favoring people who praise you but refusing to see goodness in those who disagree with you."

Confucius sighed and said, "Once I was honored in the state of Lu and held a position in the government. But treachery within the court caused me to be exiled and cursed. As far as I know, I tried to avoid the intrigues and plots, yet I was still a victim of them. How can I escape from something that is beyond my control?"

The old fisherman said, "The moment you set your foot in the political arena, you'll be entangled in the politics. You who tried to teach benevolence should know that. If you had held on to the truth and had handed political matters to those who were meant to deal with political affairs, you would not have fallen victim to political entanglements."

Confucius felt ashamed and asked humbly, "Honored sir, please tell me what do you mean by truth?"

The old fisherman said, "Truth is purity and sincerity at their highest. Those who lack purity and sincerity will not be able to persuade others. Those who show tears but feel no sadness will never experience true grief and compassion. Those who raise their voice and pretend to sound authoritative will never command respect. Those who force themselves to smile but never feel affection will never create solidarity. True authority need not be accompanied by a loud voice, true sadness and compassion are not necessarily accompanied by tears, and true harmony is not dependent on a smile. When you embrace truth within, your spirit will move among things externally and internally."

"When truth manifests itself in the family, it is loving care and gratitude. In service to a leader, it manifests as loyalty and integrity. In celebration, it manifests as joy and spontaneity. In mourning, it manifests as grief. We can say that truth is that which is the most important part of any experience. Thus, the most important thing in service is loyalty and integrity. In celebration, the most important thing is joy and abandon; in mourning, it is grief; in relating to family, it is loving care. Seek truth in the activity you are engaging in. Otherwise you'll get bogged down with petty details. Therefore, in caring for family, you should not be picky about where the money comes from as long as it is through ethical means. At festive occasions, it is more important to ensure that everyone is having a good time rather than worrying about where to get cups and dishes. When you grieve, the important thing is to feel the loss rather than squabbling over what exact funeral rite should be used.

"The sage models himself after the Way, values truth, and is not constrained by the petty and the vulgar," he added. "The ignorant person ignores the wider view of things and gets caught up with small concerns. Plodding along with everyone else, he prefers the mentality of the mob and never gets a glimpse of the limitless."

Confucius stood, bowed twice before the old fisherman, and left with his students. On the road, one of his devoted students, Zilu, asked his teacher, "Sir, you are honored among teachers. Many bow to you in respect, but we see you bowing before this rough and uneducated fisherman. Why should you give this old guy such respect?"

Confucius replied, "Zilu, have you not learned anything from the old fisherman's words? To meet someone wiser than you and fail to show respect violates etiquette. To be able to listen to the teachings of someone whose thoughts are loftier than yours and fail to show honor is to lack integrity. The old fisherman never told people to bow before him, yet those who have a glimpse of truth will recognize him as a sage and will bow in his presence.

"Those who don't see this are unfortunate indeed. You, who had the fortune of meeting a sage, threw away teachings that many would give away a fortune to receive. The truth is the Way. All things are created from it; all things dissolve into it. To go against it is to go against life; to go with it is to follow the natural order of creation. When you encounter the teaching of the Way, you need to respect it. This old fisherman certainly possesses the Way. How do I dare not show respect?"

## LIEZI

Liezi was a respected teacher, and his house was often crowded with students. Once his teacher Baiyun visited him and saw the number of shoes left outside the cottage. He turned and, without a word, walked away. Liezi ran after his teacher and said, "Teacher, you have come a long way for a visit. Please come into my house and teach me."

Baiyun said, "I won't teach you because you haven't even learned what I taught you last time. I told you that you'll have no trouble getting people to listen to you. Your problem is your inability to let them go. You say what people want to hear, happy that you have pleased them at the end of the day and hoping they will return the next day. You think you have achieved a lot by getting yourself a crowd of students.

"But no matter what you say, the clever ones tire themselves out, the anxious ones get more worried, and the petty ones don't stop their scheming. At this rate, it's better if you and your students never meet at all! Then the whole lot of you can wander around leisurely, drifting here and there, floating like an empty boat with the currents, and not be entangled in the plots and schemes of the world."

Liezi took his teacher's advice, dismissed his students, and shut himself in a retreat for three years. After that, he neither taught nor traveled. Instead, he stayed at home, cooked, cleaned, and did other chores around the house. In this simplicity, he lived out the rest of his life.

In our world today, there are many who think that they alone are right. Eager to argue and debate, they can't wait to pit their wit and cleverness against others. But those who truly possess virtue are not even aware of it, and those who walk in the Way are completely oblivious to it. They are only doing what is natural to them. The sage rests when it's appropriate and acts when it is necessary. Many people, however, do the opposite: they rest when they don't need to and push when they really need rest. To know the Way is easy; to not dwell on it is hard. The sage considers what is believed to be inevitable, transforms it into the evitable, and therefore does not have to resort to force to solve problems.

Nowadays, many consider what is evitable inevitable; therefore, they rely on force to attain results. Those who see violence as a means will always fight to make things go their way; those who refrain from violence will allow the natural way to run its course. The former ties the knots tighter; the latter allows the knots to disentangle themselves. But the best way is to not let the knots form in the first place.

The petty and greedy person sees only gifts, calling cards, and advantages. He wastes energy on shallow and trivial things but outwardly tells everyone he wants to save the world. His desire for little favors will only bring him punishments as he exploits tax loopholes, creates false documents, and schemes to cheat government, colleagues, friends, and even family. The external punishments of prison and fines will bear down on him, but it is the internal punishments of offending yin and yang, tiring body and mind, that will eat him up alive.

Confucius once said that the human mind is more dangerous than high mountains and fast rivers and is harder to understand than the ways of heaven and earth. Whereas heaven and earth follow cycles of growth and renewal, the mind is volatile and sneaky. The seasons do not lie—in spring the flowers bud; in autumn the leaves fall. However, humans may display benevolence and kindness but harbor bad intentions. In public, they may appear firm and trustworthy, but privately they are lazy and dishonest. They may look like they are organized and decisive but actually be fickle and scatterbrained. The crowd flocks to people who speak eloquently about promises, admiring their charm and drinking in their sweet talk, only later to be burned by deceit and lies.

It is for these reasons that enlightened leaders will send a subordinate on a distant mission to test loyalty and give another a position close at hand to test respect. They will give a difficult task in order to observe how well a subordinate sticks to it. They will give financial responsibilities and observe how honestly a subordinate deals with wealth. They will try to get subordinates drunk and watch how they handle themselves. They will put them in the company of sophisticated people to see how well they can hold their own. By applying these tests, a wise leader can determine whether a candidate is worthy of a position in business or in government.

If you think that you have embraced virtue, you will always consider yourself to be right and denigrate those who hold different opinions. There are certain qualities that will get you into trouble if you display them. First, being perceived as fortunate—having good looks, wealth, and influence—will make you the target of those who are failures. Second, being perceived as wise and knowledgeable will make you the target of those who are ignorant and closed-minded. Third, being perceived as brave and decisive will make you the target of those who are cowardly and fearful. Finally, being perceived as benevolent, kind, and considerate will make you the target of those who are petty and mean. Thus, the enlightened ones never displayed their wealth, fortune, knowledge, wisdom, bravery, and benevolence. Since their actions naturally follow their inborn nature, virtue is already embedded in their actions. Is there any reason to display your virtue to convince the world you are virtuous?

## UNDER HEAVEN

In ancient times, people lived according to the Way. Where does the Way come from? I say it is nowhere and everywhere. Where does en-

lightenment come from? I say that it does not need to come from anywhere because it is always there to begin with. Where do virtues come
from? The sages give birth to them; the enlightened leader completes
them. Those who do not abandon the Way are called realized beings;
those who abide in purity are called the virtuous ones. The Way is the
source of being, virtue is the root of being, and enlightenment is the
gate of action. Those who are at one with both transformation and constancy are called sages.

Those who use benevolence for inspiration, who let integrity guide
their actions, and who incorporate music and ritual into their everyday
lives are honorable men and women. The ruler who uses the principles
of enlightened leadership to establish laws and regulations, to make decisions and plan actions, and to assign appropriate people to the right
tasks are vigilant in repairing roads, dams, and irrigation ditches; they
give food and shelter to the needy, make sure that the citizens are nourished and cared for, and are the enlightened leaders of humanity.

Sages, honorable men and women, and enlightened rulers all have
this in common: they see themselves as the caretakers of the earth and
its inhabitants; they bring harmony to the nations, and they extend their
bounty and fortunes to all. Today, people do not understand that realizing the sage within is the foundation of leadership. They don't see that
the enlightened leader in public is the manifestation of the sage within.
Confused and deluded, they choose to abandon the Way. Petty and arrogant, they follow their desires, make their own rules, and impose their
beliefs on others. If they are wealthy, instead of valuing simplicity they
drown themselves in extravagance. Instead of using virtue as a standard
by which to measure their thoughts and actions, they govern their lives
by greed and ambition. Instead of aiding others in times of crisis, they
criticize those who inspire peace and harmony as weak and cowardly.
Preferring force to yielding, they are indeed far from the Way.

Not to be tempted into using vulgar means for the sake of conve-
nience, not to show off their wealth, not to bring suffering and hardship to others, and not to curry favors from the crowds, but to seek
peace and prosperity for the world, to ensure that no one goes hungry
and destitute, to know contentment, and to be pure and honest in everything they did—this is what the sages did in propagating the Way
on earth. To act for the good of all and not be partisan, to be unbiased
and just, and not to give in to the whims of the mob and interest

groups—this is what the enlightened rulers did in propagating the art of the Way in government.

Discarding flowery knowledge, doing away with the importance of self, not forcing your will on others, and not meddling with the natural course of things are the principles of the Way. Don't be too serious and pedantic, but at the same time don't be too cavalier. Take out the corners and file down the rough edges so that you can tumble and turn with the ten thousand things. Go beyond acceptance and rejection. Don't get stuck on what came before, and don't be anxious over what will come afterward, but rest in the immediacy of the present. If you don't scheme, you will not invite perils. If you don't look for praise or recognition, you will not tangle with the jealous and the petty. If you rest in stillness, you will never lose clarity and good judgment. A large tree will be knocked down by a storm, a shrub with pretty flowers will be picked clean, and bushes with juicy-looking fruits and berries will be denuded. However, a tree that looks ugly and gnarly will escape loggers, dull and unattractive flowers will not be plucked, and fruits that look dry and uninteresting will not be harvested.

To regard the Source as pure, to blend with the coarse and shun the shiny, to regard hoarding as poverty, to live in peace and contentment, and to abide in the radiance of stillness rather than the glamour of the world—these are the arts of the Way. For those who practice the arts of the Way, gentleness and humility are their outer marks, and respect for all things is their inner essence.

When you are not preoccupied with yourself, then things will reveal their true nature to you. Let your movement be as fluid as water, your stillness be like that of a mirror. Laozi said, "Know the male, but never let go of the female. Become the gully and not the ridge. Know purity but do not abandon practicality. Strive for the valley and not the peak. When others push their way to the front, stay at the rear. When others lag behind, go forward. Where others hoard, embrace that which is empty. Where others tire their bodies and minds for achievement and profit, be easygoing and leisurely. Use profundity as your root and simplicity as your guide.

"If you are too brittle, you'll be broken. If you are too sharp, you'll be blunted. Always be generous and accommodating. Inflict no pain on others. Keep yourself from being twisted by trends and fashions. Trendy clothes are discarded when they lose their glamour; fashionable ideas will be replaced when they no longer attract interest. The Way, however, stays around, because it is timeless."

Zhuangzi expounded the Way in an odd and outrageous manner. But then, he himself was an oddball. He expressed the teachings of the Way as unadorned, free of bias, fresh, and incisive. He was not afraid to be nonpartisan. He never curried favor from the authorities or the crowds; he simply came and went with the pure spirit of heaven and earth. Although his words were sharp and wild, they never caused harm. Strange and unorthodox, his manner of teaching was never arrogant and derogatory.

Above, Zhuangzi wandered freely in the embrace of the Source. Below, he befriended those who knew no beginning and no end. His understanding of the Way was broad, expansive, profound, and penetrating. He resonated with change yet was rooted in the constant. When he spoke, his words were always valid. When silent, he was hidden and arcane. Zhuangzi was truly one who embodied the Way under heaven.